Life and Letters of

Rev. Mother Teresa Dease

*Foundress and Superior General of The Institute
of The Blessed Virgin Mary in America.*

Edited by
A Member of the Community

McCLELLAND, GOODCHILD & STEWART
PUBLISHERS   :.:   :-:   :-:   TORONTO

Printing Statement:

Due to the very old age and scarcity of this book,
many of the pages may be hard to read due to the
blurring of the original text, possible missing pages,
missing text, dark backgrounds and other issues
beyond our control.

Because this is such an important and rare work, we
believe it is best to reproduce this book regardless of
its original condition.

Thank you for your understanding.

BEATI IMMACULATI IN VIA:
QUI AMBULANT IN LEGE
DOMINI—PS. 118.

CONTENTS

CONTENTS

INTRODUCTION

O N the fifth of November, 1686, Sir Thomas Gascoigne, an English gentleman, purchased a house and garden at a place called Micklegate-Bar, in Yorkshire, and deeded it to a select religious community of English ladies established in the City of Munich, Bavaria.

Some of the members were voluntary exiles who had left England during the turbulent reign of James I and entered the Community that they might in peace and security, answer the call of their Divine Master to a life of prayer and contemplation.

The foundress of this Community was the illustrious Mary Ward, an English lady, intimately associated by birth with many of the great Catholic families of Yorkshire, England. She was born on the twenty-fifth of January, 1583, in Yorkshire, and, during the dark days following the apostasy of Henry VIII, lived with her parents in Paris, France. Here, in the twenty-fourth year of her age, she founded her Community and opened at St. Omer, 1609, a select school for young ladies. The Community increased in numbers, and in time was able to answer appeals to open schools in Bavaria, Flanders, Austria and Italy. In 1642, the saintly Mary Ward visited Heworth, England, where she died on the twenty-third of January, 1645.

INTRODUCTION

Meanwhile, the religious society which she had founded continued to prosper and, increasing in numbers, opened houses in many continental cities. At Munich, these consecrated ladies established a training school for the daughters of the nobility of Bavaria. The discipline and code of rules drawn up by Mary Ward was approved by the Archbishop and, at his urgent request and on the appeal of the Duke of Bavaria, received the approbation—1703—of the reigning Pontiff, Clement XI. In 1877, Pius IX renewed the approbation and confirmed the official name of the Community, fixing as a permanency its ecclesiastical title "Institute of Mary."

From this House in Bavaria came—1686—to Micklegate-Bar, York, England, the brave and saintly few who re-established Community life and helped to save the Church in England.

This Micklegate Convent—by providential interposition or by the influence of some one near the throne—escaped suppression and confiscation during the terrible penal days, and continued for many years to train the daughters of English Catholics to high ideals, and in all the accomplishments, refinement and Christian amenities which appeal to cultured minds. From this refined home of the Community there radiated rays of light which illuminated the religious darkness shrouding the reigns of William III and Queen Anne. In 1821, Archbishop Murray, of Dublin, invited the Sisters of the Institute at Micklegate to open a Convent at Rathfarnham, in his diocese. In

INTRODUCTION

obedience to the prelate's wishes, Frances Ball, a distinguished member of the Community, accompanied by three other Sisters, sailed for Ireland and founded Loretto Abbey, near Dublin. It was named after the historic shrine of Loretto, Italy, and from this Abbey the title has, by common consent, become identified with the Institute in English speaking countries, and its members are now known, wherever the English language is spoken, as "Loretto Nuns."

Answering an invitation from the Bishop of Toronto, Rt. Rev. Dr. Power, Rev. Mother Ignatia Hutchinson, accompanied by three Sisters and a young novice, sailed from Ireland, and on September 16th, 1847, landed at Toronto. The saintly superior, worn out by the vicissitudes and severity of a rigourous climate and by trying conditions, died early in March, 1851. She was succeeded in office by Rev. M. Teresa Dease, whose life and letters, written and edited by a Sister of Loretto Abbey, Toronto, are now, for the first time, given publicity.

An impulse to record an appreciation of a refined and saintly personality and to perpetuate her beloved memory led to the compilation of this work. Those of us now living, who knew Mother Teresa, will rejoice that her letters are placed in our hands, for they will assist us in interpreting her beautiful character with more accuracy and at close range. To readers of this volume who were not privileged to know her, but only to have heard of her, these letters of a most spiritual and devout religieuse will be a spiritual tonic.

11

INTRODUCTION

Mother Teresa was a model of gentleness, of love and kindness; she was a safe guide to high ideals, and, from her childhood, was dowered with a benignity, tenderness and holiness which poured light into life and made joy more joyous. Her mental and spiritual endowments were of the finest and most delicate texture and the rich attributes of her mind seemed, to those who knew her well, only inferior to the warmth and generosity of her large and tender heart.

She possessed that peculiar quality which has been called the Science of the Saints, for to a safe and prudent asceticism she united a singular gift of penetration, and a knowledge of the workings of grace in the souls of those habitually associated with her.

For the professed nuns her conversation carried a note of the highest spirituality, for the novices it partook of a holy familiarity and condescension for human weakness, while to the educated and cultured ladies, who often called at the Abbey, her speech and voice were those of one endowed with the rare qualities of sympathy, delicacy of feeling and exceptional grace of manner. Born and educated in the bosom of refinement, she was intimately familiar with all the graces and courtesies belonging to high and exclusive society. She imparted a refinement of manner and address to the young members of her Community and to the pupils of Loretto, and these accomplishments are an inheritance left to the nuns of the Institute and to the past-graduates of the Abbey.

12

INTRODUCTION

While severe and scrupulous to herself, she was ever charitable and indulgent to others. Thoughts of God and of eternity and of the things which made for union with angels and saints, were very near and dear to the heart of Mother Teresa. She lived in the white light of eternity, for she was a woman of prayer and moved habitually in what seculars would call an "atmosphere of devotion." To her, union with God was as normal as social intercourse among others; she was in many ways a consecrated woman, the overmastering unity of whose life was established by the indwelling of the spirit of God—the Holy Ghost—in her soul. In the morning of her life she gave herself to God, she gave to Him her best in thought, in aspiration, in effort, in hope; and the oblation brought to her, as to other holy souls, abundant spiritual life, supernatural wisdom and abiding trust in God.

Far from the sepulchre of her father's repose the ashes of the good and gracious Mother Teresa; but her grave is not among strangers, her body rests in consecrated ground surrounded by the bodies of those who in life were her spiritual children and in death are not separated from her. Her memory is cherished by all who honour true womanhood, value sanctity, or love virtue. Her name will for all time be held in benediction by the nuns of Loretto who inherit from her the legacy of gracious manners, womanly refinement and culture which, to-day, adorn and distinguish them.

In the "Life and Letters of Rev. M. Teresa Dease," there is an atmosphere of meditation, a pious fervour

INTRODUCTION

and the cadences of a tender voice. The chapters are, as we would expect, principally religious, but there are some that are secular and occasionally humourous. Without doubt the writing and compilation of the book was, for the author, a labour of love. Much information of an edifying nature is scattered throughout its pages and this information is imparted informally and entertainingly. The book is a most interesting biography, graphically told and written in a pleasing conversational style charming to the average reader.

DEAN HARRIS.

LIFE AND LETTERS OF
REV. MOTHER TERESA DEASE

CHAPTER I

REV. MOTHER TERESA'S BIRTH, CHILD-HOOD, FIRST COMMUNION

A S appears from the Baptismal Register of the United Parishes of St. Mary, St. Thomas, and St. George, kept in the Church of the Immaculate Conception, Marlborough Street, Dublin, Ellen Dease, daughter of Oliver and Ann Dease, was baptized according to the rite of the Catholic Church, on the 7th day of May, A.D. 1820, having had for Sponsors, William Whelan and Mary Nugent. The babe was three days old, when she received the cleansing waters of Baptism on her brow, and it was a happy coincidence, that she who was to carry the banner of the Institute of the Blessed Virgin Mary into the Western Continent, made her primal entry into the Church on the day when the First Vespers of the great miraculous Protector of that Institute, Blessed Michael the Archangel, are chanted. Hence it is not surprising that the watchword of her wholé life was, "Who is like unto God?"

Five children were born to Oliver and Ann Dease, two sons and three daughters, of whom Ellen was the eldest, and we may well imagine the joy which the advent of this child of benediction brought to her truly Christian parents. Undue importance is sometimes attached to illustrious lineage, yet in the admission of truth, there can be no error, and it must be

2 T.D.

admitted that in the matter of birth, this favoured child was singularly fortunate, for according to Dr. Hutch, "her grandsires' grandsires could be traced in long succession through the most distinguished families in the counties of Westmeath, Longford, and Cavan. Descended on the maternal side from Christopher, fourteenth Baron Delvin, there flowed through her veins the blood of the illustrious houses of Nugent, O'Reilly and Dease, and she was the near kinswoman of Count Nugent, whose ancestors rose to high positions in the Austrian Empire, whither they were forced to flee, in order to preserve their faith, during the dark and dreary days of persecution in Ireland. The fame of Nugent's Horse was won on many a hard fought field in Flanders, during the wars of Marlborough, and bravest where all were brave, the sword of John Nugent of Ballinacor flashed victory on that bloody day, when the serried ranks of England's choicest veterans reeled before the sabre blows of the Irish Catholic exiles, on the slopes of Fontenoy."

A great deal was claimed for heredity in those days, and doubtless the appointment of Oliver Dease to the Royal British Navy—one of the first Catholics to enjoy the privilege, was a recognition of the distinguished valour of his family. The happy father of the five interesting, beautiful children, must have looked forward to many years of bliss in the home circle, but the account of his stewardship was soon to be rendered. No matter what may be the claims of affection, the summons of the King must be heeded, and preparation for the Heavenly Court brooks no delay once the fiat has gone forth. Some writer has said that "life is all chequered with sorrows and woes which chase one another like waves of the deep," and so the sunshine that flooded the cradle of the Dease children was soon followed by a dark cloud, and the happy home was shrouded in mourning for the well beloved father. What the loss of this father in early manhood signified to his family we can well imagine and the double bereavement of the little ones soon after, who lost both parents within a week of each other. But God is ever mindful of His own, the hairs of our heads are numbered, and not a sparrow falls to the ground without His knowledge, so, in His loving Wisdom; what seemed a heavy blow to the orphans, was merely a closer clasping of them in His fatherly arms.

The care of the children now devolved on their Grandmother, and most nobly must she have acquitted herself of the charge; for while many instances are not recorded of her kindly concern for them, yet there are not wanting striking proofs, that she moulded their young lives to the love and worship of their Creator; for in the revolving years, two of the daughters became Religious and Saints. Her zeal for the spiritual welfare of her young charges may be noted in an incident in the childhood of Ellen, which, although looked on at the time, as simply amusing, may in a certain sense, regarded from the aftermath of that childhood, seem prophetic. The Grandmother's idea was that children should be brought to assist at Mass. before any penalty was incurred for not attending at the celebration of the Holy Sacrifice, and so taking her precious little darling with her, one hot sultry Sabbath, after having instructed her to behave very reverently, once within the walls of the Church she forgot the child's presence and became absorbed in her devotions. Great was the old lady's dismay, when, as the priest was taking the ablution, she heard a firm small voice beside her, with all the gravity of six summers, address him, "O man, man, do not drink it all! Give me some." "Out of the mouths of babes and sucklings Thou hast perfected praise." And who knows but the language of the little one had a deeper meaning than the shocked old lady imagined, and shocked she must certainly have been, for children in the Old Land are taught that no excuse avails at any time, for breaking in on the solemnity that surrounds the Tabernacle.

The reverence for children was very marked in Ellen in her mature years, which shows what an innocent, pure heart she must have possessed in her tenderest youth. Her angelic face seemed to bear the stamp of grace, and it was believed she had never lost her baptismal innocence, for though possessed of great beauty, it was not so much the beauty of her face as the spiritual expression of her countenance that impressed one. This expression seemed to be the reflection of a soul always united to God. Later on, when many years a Religious, on one occasion the little sister of one of the Novices, brought the newly received Nun a large bouquet of rare flowers, and being instructed that her sister was in the Reception room with several Nuns and their friends, she entered with her floral gift, and bravely marched up to Reverend Mother and presented her offering. Questioned as to whom she made the presentation, the little one immediately replied, "To the Nun that looks like Our Lord." She had evidently recognized a spark of the Divine in the lovely face that was marred by no trace of passion. But Ellen had in her childhood the ways of a child, and perhaps a little of the wilfulness, for we are told that on another occasion when a mere tot she was denied some trifling favour by her Grandmother, for sitting in the same room with the august lady, she thought well to communicate her frame of mind, not to her, but to a little kitten which she stroked fondly, and with child wisdom solemnly addressed in the following manner, "There's someone in this room I do not like, and it's not you, pussy, and it's not me, pussy." Honesty found a safety valve in the kitten and Grandma might draw her own conclusions, and open negotiations for the peace that was to follow.

The gentleness which marked her every action through life must certainly have been acquired in early childhood, for it seemed a part of her very being, and had a far reaching influence on all with whom she came in contact. Gratitude to those who watched over her tender years, although not spoken in many words, seemed to be deeply enshrined in her soul, and her reverence in even pronouncing their loved names was quite marked. The affliction which the early death of her parents had been to her in her tender years, must have been a blessing in disguise, for it prepared her for the splendid self-reliance, or rather, reliance on God, which was a marked characteristic of her whole life. The reception of her First Holy Communion was an event of so sacred a character, that she was never heard to utter a word of the intimate communication of God with her soul on the morning when she made to the King of Kings the irrevocable offering of her whole heart. But one could judge from her solicitude in having children properly instructed for the reception of the Divine Guest, how fervent must have been her own preparation to receive her God, and what graces must have been bestowed on her on that eventful morn. Indeed on her deathbed the only cause of worry that seemed to disturb her, was, that a girl of thirteen years of age who had begun to receive instructions in the First Communion Class, had gone home for a holiday, and had not returned at the appointed time. To avoid giving the sufferer pain, the Religious tried to conceal the fact of the child's non-attendance; yet to her repeated inquiries a truthful answer had to be given, with the result, doubtless, of more fervent prayers reaching the Throne of Grace for the wayward child. Every period of life's existence comes to an end, but so gently, and often so gradually that, without seeming effort, one phase is merged in another unnoticed, and the toys of childhood are dropped from the hands, only that the same hands may more readily grasp the books that contain information to meet the calls of life.

CHAPTER II

GIRLHOOD, EDUCATION, VOCATION, MARY WARD, FRANCES BALL

"HOW beautiful were the days of France," says a French poet. How really beautiful life in the old world, must have seemed to this brilliant girl, who, emerging from childhood, had the protection and companionship of a beloved aunt, Mrs. Conry of Dublin. Everything that could possibly be done to render Ellen's life bright and pleasant was lovingly done by her devoted relatives, who were fully aware of the rare virtues of the soul entrusted to them. But while cherishing the spiritual tendencies manifested by the young girl, no opportunity was lost to train her for the social position in the world she seemed destined to grace, and so she was soon introduced to the society of the elect, then enjoying the morning of life in that rare old capital of her native land. At times, the home life of Dublin with its genial companionship and virtuous setting, was exchanged for the country air, and bright skies of Lisnadarra; and the return to city life, made the change which gives a variety of scene so greatly desired by the young. How cultured must have been that early environment, it was not difficult to tell in after years, and how joyous that period of her existence, which left the calm, radiant expression that lighted up her face till death. Her education— a matter of the deepest concern to those to whom she was entrusted—was well attended to, in the Metro-

23

polis where the best advantages were then obtained, and where the religious and intellectual mind was best developed.

How thorough must have been the instruction she then received in the studies she pursued, was evident to the last day of her life. Ruskin's idea seems to be, that whatever a woman learns, she should thoroughly master, and he inclines to the belief, that for one of the gentler sex, a limited area of knowledge that is accurate is preferable to a wider field carelessly gone over. But anyone who in the after years ever knew the foundress of the Institute of the Blessed Virgin Mary in America, could never imagine her doing or learning anything in a half hearted fashion. Ellen Dease learnt much and well. Her French accent and pronunciation were a marvel to natives of that land who can excuse anything rather than the murdering of their beautiful language by strangers. Her fluency of speech in that tongue was acquired by long practice in conversation with her French governesses. Italian she spoke equally well, and it was a supreme delight to her to be able to give some assistance to clergymen who had devoted their earlier years more to the study of Latin and Greek than to that of modern languages. Her musical education was thorough, and in the years that were to come, her refined taste which was pleased only with the best, elevated the standard of compositions taught in the schools, for she appreciated only what was classic.

A casual or indifferent onlooker, during the time of her scholastic training, would have judged that the young lady was being carefully prepared to adorn

some lofty position in the world, for the means to the
end were in evidence; and the brilliant mind and
graceful form left no doubt that the future held golden
hours for their possessor. But all this was exterior,
and God, Who had so richly dowered this fair
creature, had quite other designs on the loving heart
that was already entirely His in affection and in truth.
While the sun was high in the serene heavens, and
there was not the suspicion of a cloud, she chose, like
Mary, the better part which was not to be taken from
her. All her talents and facilities for education were
only the means of linking her more closely to God,
and of winning souls to His service. How meet it
was that the corner stone of the temple of Catholic
female education should have been chosen by her,
placed and polished with exquisite care. Nevertheless,
little did she dream in her happy girlhood period of
existence, that she was soon to be a pioneer in the field
of education of young girls in the New World, and
that Toronto, the Queen City of the West, was looking
across the seas, ambitious for the culture of old
Europe for her daughters. But Ellen's day dreams
then were all of the happiness of a religious life in
her home land, and the utter vanity of the world. With
St. Aloysius she turned her eyes heavenward and
said:

"What's power, what's wealth, what's sceptre's sway,
  Why seek I toys?
They're shadows all, they fleet away,
  Give me eternal joys."

And so with the eyes that regarded the things beyond,

she sought and found in the Institute of Mary the happy haven of her religious aspirations.

The Institute of the Blessed Virgin Mary, the friutful vine planted by God's own Hand in the vineyard of the Church during the days of persecution in England, founded on the Cross and bearing the precious fruit of the Cross—the knowledge of God and salvation of souls, owes its origin after God to the strong faith, firm hand, brave heart, and heroic virtue of a noble, delicate, God-fearing woman, Mary Ward. The story is now well known how, at a time when Catholics in England suffered tortures and death for conscience sake, God inspired this noble woman to leave her home and kindred early in the seventeenth century, to seek an asylum in a foreign land, where she might serve God in peace, and form the nucleus of an Institute to which the higher classes of English Catholics to which she belonged, might send their children without peril to their faith.   Her stay at St. Omer with its crucible of suffering, her return to England where God seems to have further enlightened her on the work to be done for Him, and the sufferings that would accrue therefrom, her departure again for the Continent, with a band of chosen souls, and the spread of the Institute from St. Omer to other parts of the Continent are matters of history.   St. Mary's Convent, Micklegate Bar, York, is one of the very few Catholic institutions, which survived the storm of persecution raised against the Church in England, after Protestantism had been fairly established; and, after the lapse of centuries, it still holds the place as the home whence emanates true culture, inspired by the tenets of our Holy Faith. To that venerable Institution in 1803 came a little child in her tenth year, from her dearly loved home in Dublin, to be trained in the refined Christian manner, which was characteristic of that famed Convent even in those far off days. For in those penal times there was no provision made for the education of Catholic girls of the upper and middle classes in Ireland, and to Mr. and Mrs. Ball the Bar Convent was well and favourably known, owing to the fact that their elder daughters had been educated there, with results entirely satisfactory to these good parents who sacrificed the promptings of parental affection to the claims of religious duty.

So, one bright fair morning, little Frances Ball waved adieu to her Celtic home and boarded the packet in Dublin Bay that was to convey her to the land so loved by Mary Ward, and to the Institute that resulted primarily from Mary's heroic struggles and labours. But she was not as a stranger in a strange land, for on arriving at her destination the first to greet her, after the Religious of the Institute, was her sister, Anna Maria, who was on the point of leaving school, and who suggested a walk in the garden after luncheon where the conversation that meant so much to an impressionable child drifted to another world and the elder sister addressed little Frances in the memorable words, "Seek ye, therefore the Kingdom of God and His justice, and all other things shall be added unto you." Solemn words to be addressed to a mere child, but who knows how far reaching may have been the effect? Longfellow says,

27

REV. MOTHER TERESA DEASE

"The thoughts of youth are long thoughts," and doubtless, far down the vista of life, the child looked with
dreamy, thoughtful eyes into an unknown future. The
realization of the hidden meaning of her sister's words
must have partly dawned on Frances, when on June
16th, 1805, she received the Holy Eucharist for the
first time Five blissful years spent at St. Mary's
Convent, followed by **her** return home to mourn the
death of her father, and less than four years passed
in condolence with her devoted mother, completed the
girlhood of the Irish foundress.

The story is told of the mysterious, almost miraculous manner, that the way was opened for this heroic
young lady to part from her saintly mother, and re-
enter the religious home of her childhood, there to
renounce all things.   Mrs. Ball, who was greatly
opposed to her daughter entering a religious community, was accustomed to assist daily at Mass in the
Jesuit chapel, Hardwick Street.   It happened one
morning that owing to some accidental circumstance
the Holy Sacrifice was not offered in this church at
the usual hour, and she accordingly sought out another
in which to satisfy her devotion.   Providence guided
her steps, for in the church which she entered she
fortunately heard a sermon that terrified her not a
little on account of her opposition to her child's vocation, and, eventually, powerfully contributed to the fulfilment of her daughter's wishes. The preacher, in
forceful language, dwelt on the enormous guilt of those
parents who opposed the will of God and endeavoured
to turn away their children from that state of life to
which they feel themselves called by grace and the

voice of conscience. The words of denunciation and solemn warning sank deep into the heart of Mrs. Ball, and fearful of incurring the Divine displeasure, she, on her return home, accorded to Frances the permission she had waited and sighed for so long in vain.

Frances had already been chosen by Dr. Murray, the Archbishop of Dublin, as the instrument he considered the most fitting to carry on the work of the Catholic education of girls in his diocese. He felt sure that his spiritual child possessed all the qualities requisite for so noble a task, and to St. Mary's Convent, the hallowed home of her childhood, he applied for her admission as a member of the Institute of the Blessed Virgin Mary, with the hope of introducing in time the Community to all Ireland. Catholic Ireland, and indeed many other countries, thus owe an immense debt of gratitude to the Bar Convent, which, like the sturdy oak of the forest, has braved the storms of well nigh three centuries, and the whirlwinds of passion and hatred raised with increased violence in tempestuous times, for at the Bar Convent the future foundress of the Irish branch was received as a member of the Community on June 11th, 1814. But not only the teaching orders were benefited by this kindly spirit of religious generosity of the Ladies of the Bar, but the Sisters of Charity also had received their training at York, for Mary Aikenhead had preceded Frances Ball to the Novitiate, and there received the lessons in kindly ministrations of charity which have proved such blessings to the Irish race.

Indeed Dr. Murray had as judiciously selected the

place of training for one, as for the other, for though the special aim and object of the Institute, was, and is, the education of Catholic young ladies, still at that period the York Religious were accustomed to visit the sick poor, and on such visitations were probably accompanied by the Irish Sisters of Charity who had come to them to be formed to the Religious life in their own characteristic vocation. Frances Ball's Novitiate was a peculiarly happy one. Her mistress, the saintly Mrs. Chalmers, whose life almost from the cradle to the grave, was spent within the shadow of the cloister—to whom the practices of the religious life were familiar from her infancy, found that the Irish novice gave early promise of the perfection to which she afterwards attained. Her aptitude for the various duties of her chosen state was decidedly marked. During the period of probation her fitness for the religious state was thoroughly tested, and after having edified the York Community for over two years, a great part of which time was occupied in teaching in the schools,—a duty for which her talents and acquirements eminently fitted her, she pronounced her Vows on the morning of the ninth of September, 1816.

Her exterior duties did not interfere with the interior recollection, which marked her life as quite supernatural, and she never lost sight of the purpose for which Dr. Murray had selected her, to go forth from her friends and kindred. Dr. Murray, on his side, did not neglect making inquiries of the Superior at St. Mary's, concerning his spiritual *charge,* and sought to know the light in which she regarded the future

EDUCATION AND VOCATION

Foundress of the Institute in his diocese. He even occasionally visited York, and always returned, consoled by what he had seen and heard, and filled with the hope of the abundant blessings that this spiritual child of his would bring to her native land. No wonder that after having seen and conversed with the zealous Prelate, the young Religious was stimulated to become daily more worthy of her high vocation, and better prepared for the glorious mission to which she had been destined by Providence.

Now that Sister Teresa Ball was almost ready to co-operate with him in his grand scheme for the sanctification of the weaker sex of his flock, the difficulty presented itself to Dr. Murray of securing other efficient members to carry out his designs. The shadow of the Cross under which a Christian always rests, began to loom up in the horizon, for one of the two who offered to become Sister Teresa's companions, laid down her precious life before there was even a faint outline of the promised land. But God, Who stands in need of no particular one, when some work is to be wrought for His glory, had others instructed in the science of the Saints, able and willing to help the courageous Religious, and so we find her, nothing daunted, with a firm hand copying out the Rules and Constitutions of the Institute, which were not then printed. The neatness and accuracy with which this work was accomplished may be seen by an inspection of these papers which are religiously treasured in the archives of Loretto Abbey, Rathfarnham. The thousand and one other preparations inseparable from a life-long parting occupied her few

spare moments, and one cannot help thinking it was
well thus, for strange feelings came stealing over her
soul as the farewell "that tears the life from out
young hearts" had to be spoken.

In Dublin Dr. Murray was equally busy, for we
find that he deputed Rev. Edward Armstrong to pro-
ceed to York to accompany the little band of
missionaries to Ireland, while he was negotiating for
the purchase of Loretto House, Rathfarnham, distant
about four miles from Dublin. Once established, the
fame of Rathfarnham soon spread over all Ireland,
and the wonderful success which crowned the efforts
of Mother Teresa Ball, proved that if Dr. Murray was
neither a prophet nor the son of a prophet, he was a
truly great Archbishop, to whom India, Australia and
America are not less indebted, though in an indirect
way, than the Emerald Isle. Did he ever realize the
greatness of the work he had accomplished? Probably not, for holy men are not accustomed to look
with satisfaction on the good they have accomplished
in any field of endeavour, but are ever looking forward
to the harvest yet to be garnered. His modest signa-
ture is appended to a little document in the archives of
Loretto Abbey, Toronto, stating the date of birth,
entrance into Religion, Reception, and Profession of
Ellen Dease, the Irish Foundress in America.

In this first home of the Institute in Ireland, Rathfarnham House, afterwards known as Loretto Abbey,
so wisely selected by the great Prelate, Sister Mary
Teresa (Ellen Dease) made her Novitiate. How
excellent had been the training she there received, was
evidenced in every action of her after life; and how

fully she was impressed with the Religious spirit of Rev. Mother Ball, which meant aiming at perfection in everything, was no matter for conjecture. The spirit of loyalty to the Church is shown frequently in the correspondence of Mother Ball with Mother Teresa Dease, and sometimes the latter quoted her former Superior as saying on an occasion, "The Pope thinks so, and who knows better than the Pope?" This was the summing up of all things. The sentence has a truly Celtic ring, but what a depth of wisdom is found in it—the old blessed Faith, attachment to, and confidence in Peter. It has been said that the Holy Father, Pius IX, remarked of the Institute in Ireland, "I know it well, fruitful branch of a noble tree," and truly, the nobility of the tree and the fruitfulness of the branch are now matters beyond dispute.

Twenty-four years after St. Ignatius had taken "To the greater glory of God" for the motto of his Society, it was carried by his sons into every part of the world, so in like manner Rev. Mother Ball, while zealous for the moulding of her spiritual daughters in Christian perfection, and while imbuing them with the spirit of the Rules and Constitutions, fostered also in them that zeal for making God known and loved in other parts of the world than Ireland, although this was their first and special field of action. This devotion to the foreign missions must be a characteristic of the Celtic race, for in the past Ireland and France seem to have vied with one another in their determination to carry the Faith to the uttermost ends of the earth. Many claims were soon made on Mother Ball's spiritual and material resources, claims of which she

33

was never unmindful, when there was any possibility of attending to them. She saw with the light of Faith that He, for Whom she had made the sacrifice of subjects from the home centre, could easily replace them, and she felt a real pleasure in noting that whenever a little band went generously out to save souls on the mission, there was soon after a great influx of Postulants to the Novitiate. Her heroic daughters seemed to catch this missionary spirit, and they were ever ready to brave hardships and to face danger to promote God's glory. The exit of the little company that formed the nucleus of what Dr. Hutch styled "perhaps the most successful mission ever undertaken by Mrs. Ball's daughters," though not first in point of time of departure from the Mother House, is of first importance in this narrative, and was brought about in no extraordinary way.

CHAPTER III

FOUNDATION OF TORONTO, ON INVITA-
TION OF RIGHT REV. DR. POWER

BY a Bull of Pope Gregory XVI, dated December 17th, 1841, the division of the Diocese of Kingston was effected, and all that portion of the Province lying west of the district of Newcastle was erected into a separate diocese. On the same day Right Rev. Mgr. Power, (Vicar General of the diocese of Montreal, P.Q.) was named as first Bishop, with permission to choose the city and title of his See. This humble and holy priest did all in his power to escape the dignity and even implored his Bishop to intercede in his favour that some more worthy priest might be honoured with the mitre. His humble opinion of himself only enhanced his worth in the eyes of others. He was the unanimous choice of the Canadian Episcopacy, and was recognized on all sides as the person best fitted by his wisdom, firmness and piety for the great work of founding a new diocese. Therefore, finding all his efforts to escape the honour to be unavailing, he bowed to the will of God and prepared for the difficult task that lay before him. In accordance with the privilege granted to him, after mature deliberation he selected Toronto as his Episcopal See. His consecration took place on the 8th of May, feast of St. Michael, so memorable in the annals of the Institute, and on the 9th of May he formally named Rev. J. Y. Haye as his Secretary, and on May 16th appointed

REV. MOTHER TERESA DEASE

Father W. P. McDonnell his Vicar General. Toronto was blessed in its first Bishop, "for in him were united the piety of the recluse and the zeal and ability of the missionary, and as the event proved, the patience and courage of the martyr."

On coming to Toronto Bishop Power found himself in the midst of difficulties of no ordinary kind. His diocese covered an immense territory, and the members of his flock, in many sections, were inadequately ful-filling their duties as true children of the Church. In his own episcopal city, out of about thirteen thousand six hundred inhabitants, the Catholics numbered only three thousand, with but one priest, Rev. Father Kir-wan, (Uncle of Rev. Mother Stanislaus Liddy, the present Superior General of the Institute in America), to administer to their spiritual wants.

St. Paul's was the only Catholic Church in the city and on the Bishop's arrival it became his tem-porary Cathedral. One of His Lordship's first cares on coming to the city was to secure a suitable site for his Cathedral, and with this end in view, he instituted a weekly penny collection at St. Paul's, the beginning of a Building Fund. He finally succeeded in purchas-ing a piece of land on Church St. on which the Cathedral, Palace, and the former Loretto Convent now stand. The excavation for the new Cathedral was commenced on April the seventh, 1845, and on the eighth of May, the corner stone of the present St. Michael's Cathedral was laid by the Bishop in person. Concurrently with the Cathedral was erected St. Michael's Palace which was blessed in December, 1846. The good Bishop, who was noted for his childlike faith in God, and devotion to the Blessed Virgin, yearned with affectionate solicitude to procure religious instruction for the little ones of his flock. The harvest indeed was great, but the labourers few, so the holy Prelate's thoughts turned to the old loved land and to the Institute of the Blessed Virgin Mary, the Religious Community he was anxious to secure.

Now, in this western world of ours, there were rare souls, choice flowers not yet in bloom in God's garden, which wanted only the fostering aid of Our Lady's tender touch to burst into full blossom and bear golden fruit. In January, Bishop Power visited Europe in order to obtain additional priests for his diocese, and money for the building of his Cathedral. He also applied to Mother Ball to send some members of her Community to Toronto, to assist in the work of Catholic education, when arrangements would be made to receive them. Her promise was given, and after the Bishop's return to Canada he mailed to her the following letter:

TORONTO, June 25th, 1847.

Madam,—

I have just returned to Toronto, and I feel more convinced than ever that a branch of your Community will succeed admirably here after a short time. I cannot inform you of the number of scholars (boarders) you might have, because you are likely to have (after a few months) fifty as twenty. As soon as you are known, the good Ladies whom you intend sending out will have as much as they can do. As a matter of course, it will be my business to see, especially in commencing, that they may have no reasonable motive to complain. I shall immediately see where I can find a convenient residence, in order that everything may be ready at their arrival, or a few days afterwards, in case that I cannot learn the exact time of their coming. The day school will, I hope, be numerously attended after a few weeks, and the common school filled by a great number. However, I am aware that for a short time there may exist among the Protestants slight prejudice, but when the parents will find that they can obtain a cheaper and better education for their daughters in the Convent than in any other establishment, they will certainly avail themselves of its advantages. By requesting your Chaplain, Rev. M. Farrelly, to inquire of Roche Bros. in Dublin the day of sailing of the fastest ship of the line, you can engage the passage of the ladies immediately. A clergyman who is going to New York intends speaking to some members of the firm in order to afford you every convenience, but I am sure that by following the line I have marked out, you will not meet with the slightest difficulty in sending the good Nuns to Liverpool on the sixth of August. I find now that the boat sails on the first of July, but there are other ships in every respect as good and comfortable as "the Yorkshire," for instance the Queen of the West. I should like to know the day the ladies are to sail, and the probable date of their arrival in New York, so as to have someone on the spot to meet them. I shall write also to the Bishop of New York to request one of his priests to watch for the arrival of the ship, in order to avoid any delay or disappointment. You remember that the people (Catholics, mostly, Irish or of Irish

descent) are not rich. Some families are well able
to educate their daughters. I beg of you to write me
by the sixteenth of July or the first of August, so that
I may be fully prepared to have everything ready.   I
suppose it would be better not to furnish the house
until after the Nuns' arrival. If they have those things
which are necessary for the celebration of the Mass,
so much the better, they can bring with them in that
respect as much as they please.   Anything else can be
had here as cheap as in Ireland.

I have the honour to remain, with every feeling of
respect and regard,

Madam,
Your most obedient and humble servant in J.C.
+ MICHAEL,
Bishop of Toronto.

MRS. BALL, *Superior,*
Loretto Abbey, Rathfarnham.

As the practical outcome of this petition—a Novice
and four professed members—Mother Ignatia Hutchinson, Sr. M. Teresa Dease, Sr. M. Bonaventure
Phelan, Sr. M. Gertrude Fleming and Sr. M. Valen-
tina Hutchinson, left Rathfarnham Abbey for the far
West on the 5th of August, 1847, under the care of
Mother Ignatia Hutchinson, whom Mother Ball had
appointed Superior of the little band of missionaries.

39

CHAPTER IV

VOYAGE, ARRIVAL IN TORONTO, CHOLERA RAGING, BISHOP GREATLY DISTRESS- ED, DEATH OF BISHOP POWER

THE feast of Our Lady of Snows was the day of the heroic sacrifice of the missionaries, and amidst the tears and blessings of Rev. Mother Ball and the loved Community of Rathfarnham, they departed on their mission of love and mercy. On the way to the wharf signs of mourning were visible on all sides, and presently the sad pageant of the funeral procession of Daniel O'Connell loomed in sight. Truly not a cheering spectacle, for the liberator had been a giant in the fight for Catholic Emancipation, and although he had won many a hard fought battle in Parliament, the strife was by no means ended. After a disagreeable passage across the Channel they reached Liverpool on the sixth, in time to hear Mass at the Convent of Mercy where they were hospitably received and entertained. But notwithstanding the kindness shown them, the five days spent in the gloomy city of Liverpool must have seemed long and weary to these voluntary exiles destined for a foreign land. Bishop Power did everything possible to smooth their way across the ocean, and was exceedingly solicitous for their convenience and comfort; but from the heights of Heaven the Almighty Father, Whose work they had pledged themselves to do, had prepared for them a path resembling the Via Crucis of His well-beloved Son.

40

ARRIVAL IN TORONTO

As a prelude to the disappointments and sufferings that awaited them in America they were obliged to take passage in the sailing vessel "Garrick" instead of in either of the ships mentioned by the Bishop in his letter to Rev. Mother Ball. The voyage was unmarked by any unusual incident; the Nuns gave most of their time to the performance of their spiritual duties at the prescribed time, as nearly as they could compute, and kept their hearts lovingly united to the Divine Pilot, Who was guiding them safely over the perilous ocean. After six weeks' sailing, they reached New York on the feast of the Seven Dolours, when the Church places before her children the sad spectacle of Calvary's Mount, the agony of a mother's heart, and the undying love of the world's Redeemer. They had left Rathfarnham on the feast of Our Lady of Snows, and under her protection had reached the New World, there to be greeted by their sorrow stricken Queen. Through the kindness of Mr. Dunnigan the pious travellers were enabled to find a suitable hotel in New York, where, notwithstanding the secular dress assumed to prevent their being recognized as Religious, they were addressed as Nuns even by little children. The sail down the Hudson by moonlight had an elevating effect on their spirits, and they raised their hearts to the God Who had created such scenic beauty, for Whose sake they had left parents, and home and country. With Pharaoh's magician they could say, "The finger of God is here." From New York to Albany they travelled by the steamer, which in those early days of steam appliance seemed like a floating palace. From Albany to Rochester they went by rail,

41

suffering intensely from the cold, for which they were
totally unprepared so early in the season as the 14th
of September. The last portion of the journey was
made on the water of Lake Ontario, and the dawn
of the 16th of September revealed Toronto the
promised land.

Great was the embarrassment of the poor Nuns
when, on landing, there was no friendly voice to greet
them. They knew not in what direction to turn, but
were finally somewhat relieved by the appearance of
a coloured cabman, who offered his services to convey
them to their destination. Having with some difficulty made him understand where they wished to go,
they proceeded on their way, when to their dismay the
wheel came from under the carriage—the accident,
slight in itself and causing no damage, yet seemed a
sad portent of what awaited them at their journey's
end On their arrival at the Palace they were kindly
but sadly received by the good Bishop, on whom a
heavy gloom had already settled. The place looked
bare and oppressively lonely, and there was a sadness
in the atmosphere, which even the absence of the sun
of prosperity could not make quite intelligible. The
father of their adoption, who seemed so willing and
well calculated to be an example to them in bearing
the crosses of a missionary life, was seemingly disquieted, if not quite alarmed at their coming, which
was afterwards explained by the knowledge of the
distressing fact that typhus fever was raging in the
house, and of his very few Priests, one was lying
delirious in his room, another just convalescent—in
fact the whole city might be called a vast plague spot,

42

and the Bishop's Palace an hospital. Naturally the anxious Prelate feared for the Nuns' lives, but their entrance to Heaven was not to be so soon accomplished, "gold and silver are tried in the fire, but acceptable men in the furnace of humiliation." Shown to the rooms appointed for them, they hastened to resume the holy Habit, the sacred livery of their dear Master, which circumstances had compelled them to lay aside for so many weeks. With what satisfaction they must have laid aside the garb of the world and clothed themselves in the garments that betokened the renunciation of its vanities and pleasures. The morning after their arrival they were introduced to the Ven. Archdeacon Hay, the Bishop's Secretary, who seemed already advanced in consumption, for every feature bore witness to the ravages by the disease which was also evidenced by his almost inaudible voice. This holy man afterwards became their Confessor, indeed there was no other Priest in Toronto, except one, on whom the spiritual charge of the whole city devolved, Very Rev. Dean Kirwan, already mentioned, who was just recovering from fever. They also met for the first time Very Rev. Father Carroll of Niagara, a worthy, affable, kind hearted man, gifted with genuine Irish good humour, whose mirthful countenance and conversation contrasted strongly with the gravity and serious mien of the Venerable Archdeacon. Father Kirwan took his leave of the Bishop the morning the Nuns had for the first time the honour of partaking of His Lordship's hospitality. There was something touching in the reverence mingled with love discernible in the look and manner of the Reverend Dean as he

knelt to receive for the last time the blessing of his
beloved spiritual Father and Bishop. Little did either
then dream that it was their final parting on earth.
The poor Priest, as he left for Niagara, whither the
Bishop had sent him to recruit after the fever, was
far from imagining that the Prelate, then full of life
and prospects, would, ere many days had elapsed, fall
a victim to the very disease from which he himself
had so lately narrowly escaped. During the dinner
after the Priest's departure, the Bishop seemed far
from cheerful. His kind heart was evidently op-
pressed by the scenes of sorrow he had witnessed in
the early morning, during his visits to the hospital,
where the emigrant fever was raging. The thought
of so much suffering weighed heavily on him, he could
not eat, and his flushed cheek and restless eyes betokened the anxiety and even alarm that agitated his
mind. He did not wish to be reminded of what he
could not forget even for a moment, so that when
anyone inquired how the patients in the hospital were,
he would say, "Do not speak of them. I heard the
confessions of many to-day and anointed them." The
presence of the Nuns at such a critical period was
evidently an additional cause of uneasiness to the poor
Bishop, for he feared lest they too should become a
prey to the fell disease which had penetrated even into
his home. He was most particular about the food
that was served them, especially the fruit, lest there
should be any taint that would imperil their lives. But
the Nuns were spared for other and still greater sufferings, for the Father who had invited them and prayed
for their coming was soon called to his reward. One

midnight a message reached him that a poor woman lay dying in the immigrant shed, and was asking for a priest to assist her on her last journey. As there was no one else to answer the call, the saintly prelate, bearing the Blessed Sacrament and Holy Oils, went out into the night to fortify this poor soul to meet its Creator. He fulfilled his mission but as the event proved, at the cost of his own life, for as he came out of that pestilential abode he carried within him the seeds of the dread malady. On reaching the free, pure air, it is said he raised his eyes to Heaven, and in a voice, tremulous with deep emotion, uttered the following words, "My God, what crimes England has to answer for." Symptoms of the dire disease manifested themselves the next day. The fever developed into one of a most malignant type, the patient grew rapidly worse day by day till at last on the first of October was heard the melancholy announcement, "The Bishop is dead!" Expressions of the most heartfelt sorrow were heard on every side, and the occasion and manner of the holy man's death called for the praise and admiration of the entire Community. Terrible was the blow to the poor, sorely tried Nuns.

CHAPTER V

FIRST HOUSE OF THE INSTITUTE OF THE B. V. M. ON DUKE ST. FIRST MASS SAID THE FOLLOWING MORNING. SCHOOLS OPENED. SYMPATHY AND KINDNESS OF TORONTO LADIES

WHAT the good Bishop's illness and death meant to the exiled Nuns can scarcely be imagined, but meanwhile they had opened the first house of the Institute of the Blessed Virgin Mary on Duke St. on September 24th, feast of Our Lady, Queen of Mercy, A.D. 1847, and assisted at the first Mass in their new home on the following morning. The classes were begun on the 29th of September, a blissful augury, the feast of the great Archangel, Michael. The Bishop was buried on the 5th of October, and Sister Teresa Dease, who was appointed to preside at the first recreation in the boarding school, had a truly difficult part to sustain. She, who could not realize how the birds could sing and the sun could shine, when her heart was so sad, was obliged to enter into the spirit of the occasion, and endeavour by cheerfulness to render those around her happy, to make them feel content after they had left their home and parents to come among strangers, whose unfamiliar faces and strange costume served to make their dear pupils feel anything but at home. During the first recreation, or rather attempt at it, the funeral cortege passed. As the Cathedral was not roofed in, the mourning procession first proceeded to St. Paul's Church where the solemn service for the dead was held, and the people allowed to pay their last tribute of respect to the departed martyr, after which the remains were conveyed to their last resting place under the new Cathedral. The blow had indeed well nigh crushed the hope of the brave little band, but quickly recognizing that it was the will of God they looked on this first great trial as an incentive to adhere more closely to the great Father in Heaven, Omniscient and Omnipotent, and "Whose mercy endureth forever." Many a subsequent sorrow seemed to re-echo in moments of trial the sad announcement, "The Bishop is dead!" In some grief was suppressed, in others and in the Mother Superior particularly, sorrow for the death of the great Prelate was excessive and made itself clearly perceptible, but whether buried in the deep cells of the heart or expressed in words or tears, the sorrow was an abiding one Tennyson says, "Sorrow's crown of sorrow is the remembrance of happier things," but in this case the crown was not in the remembrance of a happiness that had passed away, but in the hope that lay buried Mary had to tear herself away from the foot of the Cross, and so the members of her Institute had to face strange surroundings and apply themselves to the task their vocation demanded.

Nor were kind friends wanting to them, as the sequel will show. The Nuns were welcomed by a few of the leading Catholics in Toronto whose names have been long cherished by the Community. The Hon. Mrs. Bolton and her niece, Mrs. Crawford, two

REV. MOTHER TERESA DEASE

Catholic ladies of the highest social standing, were their first visitors, and they gave the Nuns a very favourable impression of Canadian society. Mr. and Mrs. Elmsly were their next callers, and from their conversation was gleaned the great zeal they had for religion, and their praiseworthy devotedness to the Bishop and Church. Mr. Elmsly's two daughters were among the first pupils of the Nuns, and they were followed by the two daughters of Mr. Lynn, an English convert like Mr. Elmsly, who proved to be one of the best friends of the Institute. Of these two gentlemen, the saintly successor of Bishop Power, writing to Rome some years later, said, "Two Englishmen, converts from Anglicanism, have saved the whole Catholic establishment in Toronto, by giving all their fortunes in security. I should be happy if the Holy See would grant a mark of its satisfaction to these two fervent Christians, the Hon. Capt. John Elmsly and Mr. S. G. Lynn, merchant. They resemble body and soul, those Angels of whom St. Gregory remarked, when he saw them for sale in the market place of Rome, that they would soon come to be called angels. Capt. Elmsly has gone to sea in order to gain money to help his Bishop, from which undertaking I was not able to dissuade him. He has also given me some land which I have already offered to the Reverend Jesuit Fathers in order to induce them to establish themselves here." As Canon Law fordids the consecration of a Church until it is entirely free from debt, that of the Cathedral (fifty-seven thousand, six hundred dollars) was assumed by these two gentlemen, and it was consecrated September the twenty-

48

ninth, 1848. Mrs. De la Haye, following the example of Mrs. Elmsly, placed her five daughters under the care of the Nuns, and remained a true friend to them till death. Her name is gratefully remembered in the records of Loretto. Somewhat later Mrs. P. Foy made the acquaintance of the Nuns, and when in after years her daughters entered the boarding school, Rev. Mother Teresa was pleased to remark the good lady's kindly remembrance of the Nuns in the early days. In after years a grateful smile lighted up the face of the Foundress when she announced to the Community that Mrs. Foy was coming to spend a whole day with her.

These early manifestations of sincere good will had a most cheering effect on the religious exiles, and they summoned all their energies to meet the requirements of the land of their adoption; but the time of the harvest was not yet, and more bitter tears had still to flow in the seeding, ere they were to bear their full sheaves. "They that fear the Lord will prepare their hearts and in His sight will sanctify their souls" (Ecclesiasticus). The annual eight days' Retreat, so precious to the life of every Religious, could not be made at the usual time, and the Nuns took advantage of the absence of the pupils during the first Christmas holidays to enter upon this holy exercise. It was during this Retreat, when the Nuns were enjoying a little of the sweetness of Mount Thabor, that sickness made its appearance in the little Community. Sister M. Bonaventure de Sales and Sister M. Gertrude showed symptoms of the maladies that were to bring them to an early grave, though not before they had suffered pains hardly exceeded by those of the martyrs. From the annals of Loretto may be gleaned the spiritual aid received at this time from Rev. M. Paré, Chaplain to the Nuns, whom the saintly Bishop Bourget sent to help the sorely pressed priests of Toronto, and as Chaplain to the Nuns. His successor in the office of Chaplain was Rev. Father Harkin, loaned by the Archbishop of Quebec. In 1849 the Sisters removed from the house on Duke St. to a more convenient residence on Simcoe St. Dr. Hutch, in his life of Mrs. Ball, says, that "Duke St. was the Gethsemane of the Nuns, but that Simcoe St. was to be their Calvary."

The first victim claimed by death was Sister M. Bonaventure de Sales, whose life had been so holy that for her death had no terrors. She had been suffering since the Christmas Retreat of 1847, and now her spiritual Sisters kneeling by her deathbed besought her that when she should have entered into her reward she would obtain from God some aid for the few she left behind—the Superior, Mother M. Ignatia Hutchinson, Sister M. Gertrude whose sufferings were intense, Sister M. Teresa Dease and the Novice before mentioned. On these two last mentioned Sisters every duty devolved. It would appear that the intercession of the deceased was most efficacious, for three days after her death Rev. Mother Ball, taking into consideration the great difficulties under which her Canadian children laboured, obtained the willing and generous consent of two young members of her Community to sail for Canada and accept the sorrow and suffering of the distant mission. Sister M. Bonaventure's death took place on the eleventh of

OPENING OF FIRST HOUSE OF B.V.M.

April, 1849, and on the eighteenth of the same month Sister M. Joachim Murray and Sister Ita Cummins, a lay Sister, set out for Toronto under the protection of the good Capt. Elmsly. They reached Quebec, after a stormy passage of eight weeks. The kind Ursuline Nuns sent their physician, Dr. Noet, to meet them at the wharf, and conduct them to their Convent, where they were most hospitably welcomed by the whole Community. By order of the venerable and amiable Archbishop, they were treated as distinguished guests, and many unusual privileges were accorded the Nuns in honour of their guests, the Irish missionaries. Indeed, the travellers' encomium on the charitable kindness of the Ladies of the fine old Monastery was, that it was beyond description. In Montreal, too, they were the recipients of great kindness from the daughters of the saintly Margaret Bourgeois, from whom they received most cordial hospitality.

On June the sixteenth, 1849, the tired travellers reached their home in Toronto, and who can describe the affecting meeting which then took place in that house on Simcoe St. But it was not alone in Ireland that Sister Bonaventure's intercession made itself felt, for a brighter augury than the advent of the two Irish helpers, was the entrance of the first Canadian Postulant, Sister Joseph McNamara. This lady entered the Novitiate on the eighth of May, and the help thus opportunely afforded to the struggling Community had not come one moment too soon, for Sister M. Gertrude's suffering had by this time reached an acute state. The first symptom of her malady was a small lump which appeared on her knee, and after

51

awhile her great toe was affected. As she was appointed to teach a parochial school in the city some distance from the Convent, and had to walk all the way to her work, she must have suffered agony at every step. But no murmur escaped her. Later she had charge of St. Francis Xavier's School, largely attended by children of the rising classes, among whom she effected much good by her saintly example. At last her sufferings became so great, that she could no longer walk, and she was obliged to remain at home. In such agonizing pain, it was admirable to see how the poor sufferer maintained her affability. She was even cheerful, wishing for the hour of recreation more than the other tired, though healthy Sisters, to whom it was such a boon. Although not able to attend the outside school, she did much for the Community by presiding at the study in the refectory, and at other duties. On all occasions she rendered herself exemplary by her patience, meekness, and punctuality. Indeed the most wayward and frivolous of the pupils did her the justice of saying she was a Saint. Frequent lancing of the affected parts gave no hope of a cure, and finally it was deemed expedient to remove the foot. To this painful operation Sister M. Gertrude heroically submitted without uttering a moan or even sighing until the marrow was reached, then she gently breathed the Holy Name of Jesus. In her hands was her Crucifix, the Image of Him Who had said, "I have trodden the wine-press alone, and of the Gentiles there was not a man with me." By the Divine permission—perhaps to increase her merit—the instruments made use of to perform the operation were blunt, and consequently caused her more pain than she would otherwise have had to suffer. Another aggravating circumstance in the case was, that all the diseased part was not removed, and consequently her sufferings were prolonged, until on the anniversary of Christ's Nativity, 25th December, 1850, she went to the God Whom she loved, and in union with Whom she suffered. The Chaplain, when he saw her after death, exclaimed, "Angelical soul," and the Bishop who knelt by her bedside recommended himself to her prayers with confidence as to one who had already entered Heaven. On the feast of the beloved Disciple, her mortal remains were deposited in the vaults of St. Michael's Cathedral beside those of Sister Bonaventure de Sales.

Doubtless the spiritual ministrations of the two priests afforded great consolation to the stricken Nuns at this crucial period, and enabled them to bear with fortitude and resignation the trials which Providence had been pleased to send them. Father Harkin not only provided for their spiritual wants but interested himself largely in their temporal welfare. With their schools he was specially concerned, and his efforts in bringing the excellence of their system of education before the public were most praiseworthy and fruitful of good results. It was at his suggestion that the Nuns first held public examinations at the close of the scholastic term, and these intellectual tests were followed by pleasing dramatic performances or concerts. Whatever may be the opinion to-day of the advantages or disadvantages of such entertainments, certain it is, that in those early times they were of great service to the schools. The very first families of Toronto were anxious to obtain invitations to them, and parents judged for themselves of the methods of teaching pursued by the Nuns, and of the modest, graceful manner in which the pupils acquitted themselves in those accomplishments which enter so largely into female education. The training of the heart for God was to be witnessed by His All-seeing Eye and developed in those precious lives that were afterwards to shed such radiance over their appointed spheres. But in those remote days when means of communication with the Old World were so few and primitive a reputation for the schools had to be established under the eyes of those interested; and as a natural consequence of the success of these public examinations and renditions, the number of the pupils was largely increased.

CHAPTER VI

BISHOP DE CHARBONNEL. DEATH OF
REV. M. IGNATIA HUTCHINSON. REV.
M. TERESA DEASE APPOINTED SUPER-
IOR.

THE widowed Church of Toronto had meanwhile
been three years without a Pastor, when the Holy
See appointed to the diocese Dr. de Charbonnel, a
Frenchman of noble birth, who was distinguished as
much for his virtue as for his noble lineage. He was
consecrated Bishop by Pope Pius IX in the Sistine
Chapel on May 26th, 1850, and as a souvenir of his
consecration the Holy Father presented him a well
filled purse, and a chasuble of gold cloth upon which
was embroidered the Papal Arms. In addition to
these His Holiness offered him his choice between a
fine ciborium and a rich chalice. His Lordship chose
the ciborium, then taking the chalice in his other hand
he turned towards Pius IX and said, "Quid retribuam
Domino; pro omnibus quae retribuit mihi? Calicem
salutaris accipiam et nomen Domini invocabo." The
Pope, with a smile, appreciated the apt quotation and
the Bishop withdrew, the happy possessor of ciborium
and chalice. A few days afterwards he quitted Rome
to travel through France in the interests of his diocese.
He reached Toronto September 21st, 1850, and the
following Sunday took formal possession of his See.
He was reputed to be a man fit for the heavy task
that awaited him, full of zeal, energy and patience.

He undertook courageously the liquidation of the heavy debt on the Cathedral erected by his predecessor, and consecrated in 1849, owing to the generous efforts of the two converts already mentioned. Before he was long in possession of his See, he was called upon to assist at the deathbed of the Mother Superior of the Loretto Convent. How frequent were the calls of the Angel of Death on the young Community has already been noted, and this last knock at the Convent gate was perhaps the hardest, since it took away her whom the members had been accustomed to regard with reverence and confidence. She had been ailing and delicate during Sister M. Gertrude's illness, and with difficulty dragged herself to be present at the final struggle of the heroic Sister, for she could scarcely walk a few yards at the time of Sr. M. Gertrude's death. Nevertheless like Mary at the foot of the Cross, she looked into the face of the loved one, and did not leave until the struggle was over, and she had lovingly closed the eyes of the dear child she was soon to join in Heaven.

Mother Ignatia Hutchinson's life was one of unfailing generosity in God's service, and from the annals of Loretto Abbey we learn that when there was question of extending the kingdom of Christ in the New World, on learning that she was destined for the office of Superior of the little missionary band, her humility declined the honour, and only accepted it when told by Rev. Mother Ball that no mission would go to Canada unless she consented to be its head. She took up the Cross bravely and endeavoured to carry it even to the end, though bending 'neath its weight, but, with eyes ever turned heavenward, she reached the goal to which the cross always leads. Nor was the good God unmindful of his faithful servant for he sent her spiritual aid as we have seen, and a trusty guide to cheer her on her journey, a holy Jesuit Father, the wise and saintly Dr. Tellier, who in the interest of the Community and its head, proved a worthy successor to the zealous Father Harkin. On the ninth of March Dr. King, the physician recommended to the Nuns by the Most Rev. Dr. Power, came to visit his patient, and before his departure Rev. Mother Ignatia said, "Have I many days to live, Doctor?" Without a moment's hesitation he replied, "Not one hour, lady." Immediately she called for Sr. M. Teresa Dease to light the blessed candle and say the prayers for the dying. The Bishop, as we have seen, came to bless her deathbed by his presence. The last moment drew nigh and the last blessing was given; in the presence of the Bishop and Community, and in the arms of Sr. M. Teresa, the patient, saintly sufferer calmly expired on the ninth of March, 1851. What must have been the feelings of Sister Teresa Dease, as the dead form of her loved Superior lay in her arms, and she found herself the only surviving member of that little pioneer band of professed Religious who left Rathfarnham on that memorable feast of Our Lady, August the 5th, 1847. Want, loneliness, desolation, death, seemed to be ever present with them, and now, in their direst distress not one word of direction or comfort to cheer them from that cherished home across the sea, for it took seven or eight weeks for a letter to reach them from Ireland. "Many are the afflictions of the just, but out of them all will the Lord deliver them." (Psalms.)

All that love and devotion could suggest was done to show respect to the holy dead, and for the third time in less than two years, the vaults of St. Michael's were opened to receive a child of Our Lady, where the venerated remains of the saintly Rev. Mother Ignatia Hutchinson were laid to rest. True, in her declining years, her delicate state of health had prevented her being actively engaged in teaching in the schools, but her example and saintly life were ever reminders of her union with God, and her successor was heard to say, that meeting her, even in the halls, had the effect of raising the heart of a Religious to God. Yes, it was true she had left them forever, and on her assistant, Sr. M. Teresa Dease, devolved the added responsibility of being at least temporary head of the Community. This was no small charge, although the number of her subjects was few, only six, all counted, one a lay Sister and so not available for teaching, two Novices,—the Postulant, Miss Mc-Namara, who had been received and named Sr. M. Joseph, and Miss Charlotte Lynn, Sr. M. Ignatia, who had been the first boarder in the Convent on Duke St. and the first Blue Ribbon, as the Child of Mary is designated in the schools, and who had entered on the 29th September, 1850,—besides the three professed Nuns. The offices of the Community, small though it was, had to be performed by the one experienced member, and although the greatest goodwill and energy were manifested by the new recruits, still with the teaching of English, French, Music and Drawing,

one can easily see how tired and overworked those
faithful souls must have been.

The death of the original members, and the dis-
couragement following, did not prevent subjects from
joining the Community as we have seen in the case of
Miss Charlotte Lynn, Sr. M. Ignatia, who with the
full approbation of her father (the grandson of the
Protestant Bishop of Carlisle) in her fifteenth year
renounced the world to become the bride of Christ,
and never cast "one longing, lingering look behind."
The Bishop had appointed Sr. M. Teresa Dease,
Superior temporarily, awaiting the decision of Mother
Superior at Rathfarnham, to whom he had written to
consult her wishes, and in a short time his appointment
was ratified by Rev. Mother Ball, who wrote him in
reply, "Sr. M. Teresa Dease is a person of superior
mind and distinguished piety, and our Archbishop
concurs in the opinion that she is well suited to take
the place made vacant by the lamented death of Rev.
Mother Ignatia Hutchinson. On the feast of St.
Joseph, March the 19th, 1851, Rev. Father Tellier, S.J.,
brought to the Convent on Simcoe St. the following
letter from Bishop de Charbonnel announcing the
appointment of Sr. M. Teresa Dease to the office of
Superior:

ST. JOSEPH'S DAY, 1851.

Dear and Reverend Sisters in Our Lord,—
I am happy to know by what I read and heard, that
I can with propriety confer on your beloved Sister
Teresa the title of Reverend Mother.

She did not claim it any more than she wished for

the authority, which Providence has entrusted to her devotedness, but you yourselves, true daughters of obedience, have called upon your Bishop in order to have at your head one with the sweet name of Mother, and to give your submission something filial.

Be blessed for such feelings, O dear family of Loretto, be blessed by the Holy Trinity of Nazareth. There everyone obeyed, and none commanded, there the Most Excellent was the Most Obedient, there the last was the first; there all were one in Jesus, Mary and Joseph, in Whose name I will go and bless you this evening at half past four o'clock.

. . . .

After the reading of this letter, she made the usual promises into the hands of Rev. Father Tellier, and on the same evening the Bishop visited the Convent and gave Benediction.

One can easily realize how, with so much sickness and change and death, the schools must have been interfered with, and their progress checked, and so, after the demise of Rev. Mother Ignatia Hutchinson, it was deemed prudent to send away the boarders to their homes until the following September, and so do more justice to the day school, and to the Sisters who after four p.m. were then partially free. Strange though it may seem, it has often happened that the health of an individual has been preserved under mental suffering, or over exertion or anxiety, until the disquieting cause has ceased, and then in the period of repose has come the collapse. So it was with Rev. Mother Teresa, whose strength had lasted through

60

every struggle and endured every strain, and when finally there was at least a partial release from most pressing and painful duties, she was attacked with low fever or ague so acute that the Bishop found it necessary to recommend her for change of air to Niagara. The Pastor of the mission, Rev. Father Moussart, seems to have been most kind to the invalid and her companion, and after an absence of a month she returned to Toronto much improved in health and spirits, and most favourably impressed with the health-giving properties of the air of Niagara. While everything was being made ready for the return of the boarders in September, a most valuable acquisition to the Community had been made in June, 1851, in the person of Sr. Gonzaga Donovan. On the fifth of September, the very day on which classes were resumed, Sr. M. Berchmanns Lalor and Sr. M. Purification Oullahan arrived from Rathfarnham to assist the little band that had struggled so bravely.

Needless to say with what joy they were received by their Sisters who with this reinforcement and increase in the Novitiate, hoped to do great things for the glory of God, which they eventually did as the sequel will prove. The following letter of thanks from Rev. Mother Teresa to Rev. Mother Ball shows how fully the kindness of the Irish Foundress in sending these two Sisters was appreciated.

LORETTO HOUSE, SIMCOE ST.,
TORONTO, 15th Sept., 1851.

Very Dear Rev. Mother,—

I thank you in the name of all for all you have done

for us in sending to our aid the two members you so justly prized. They arrived safe, after a long and stormy passage, and are now quite happy in their trans-Atlantic home. You will be glad to hear that one of these dear Sisters remarked that the customs here are perfectly conformable to those observed in Ireland. Our prospects now are very good, thank God. All are in good health and spirits. I am not strong, but am much better than I have been for some time past. We expect to have two Receptions on the twenty-sixth of this month, and two Professions in November. The dear Sisters have entertained us delightfully by their accounts of the peace, virtue and consequent happiness of the home they have left. I rejoice to hear that you are so well, dearest Rev. Mother, may you long continue so. You were most kind to mention Mother Mary Columba and Sr. Mary Eucharia in whom I feel interested. Their early years gave promise of what you now esteem in them. I seldom have the satisfaction of hearing directly from Sr. M. Eucharia, but I am quite resigned, knowing that she is most happy under the more than maternal protection of the kindest of mothers. I shall write soon again, giving you an account of the distribution of offices and earnestly begging your prayers and blessings.

> I remain,
> Dear Reverend Mother,
> Your devoted child in J. C.,
>
> MARY J. TERESA.

APPOINTED SUPERIOR

Some writer says that "only the toilers know the sweetness of rest and calm," and this may possibly be true, but equally true it is that there is a joy in activity, and this joy is enhanced when the exertion will obviously benefit someone outside the agent or actor in the drama. So, although only five of the boarders who had been dismissed on that sad morning of the ninth of March, made their appearance in the Convent on Simcoe St. on the following fifth day of September,—the opening—still the hopes of the Mistresses ran high for the rich harvest they saw in the far future that must one day be garnered. Great things are generally, though not always, accomplished slowly—one by one the first stars are seen until presently a galaxy appears—the increase of the boarders was slow but sure, and the interest of the people of Toronto, which seemed to wane while the cloud lasted, began again to be awakened; and to the efforts the missionary band put forth, under the influence of their abiding faith, a hearty response seemed at last to be given. Sister M. Teresa Corrigan was the fourth Postulant to enter, and from the annals already quoted we learn how she accompanied Sister Joseph McNamara to the day school on Church St., two miles distant from the Convent, and that neither rain nor snow prevented their regular attendance at their post of duty, although the distance was always travelled on foot. A rather amusing story is told of the former of these two Sisters. Sister Teresa Corrigan, young and innocent, who had embraced the Religious life in her sixteenth year, and who had heard or read in the lives of the Saints so much of the dangers of the outside world which she had never known, that when she was appointed to take the young ladies for their daily walk, she hesitated to accompany them until Rev. Mother Teresa reassured her of her safety while acting under obedience, and meanwhile placed a relic round her neck.

CHAPTER VII

CONVENT ON BATHURST ST. PROGRESS OF INSTITUTE. MISSION TO BRANTFORD.

TOWARDS the close of the year 1852, the Nuns transferred their residence to Bathurst St., St. Mary's parish. Here they had already established a Parochial school which was largely attended, and from that time forth success seems to have attended their every effort. The house itself was in no way attractive, nor even particularly comfortable, but it was large and roomy, and somehow the Nuns came to the conclusion that it would benefit the health of all, and this forecast tended to improve their spirits. However, there is no reckoning on when or where the grim visitant will make his appearance, and even here his knock was distinctly heard after a short period. This time it was Sr. Magdalen Shea death claimed, a dear young creature, pious and talented, who had entered with the highest hopes of working for God and the Institute. She had charge of the Parochial school and was devoted, heart and soul, to this labour of love. Wide and all-embracing were her plans for the little ones for whom she laboured, when gradually her health began to fail, and she had to bow to the will of her Creator Whose fiat had gone forth that here her labours were soon to end. During her short time of probation she was never known to show by word or look the slightest objection to any order of

65

obedience, and so when the final summons came, before her probation was ended, she was ready to meet the Bridegroom. She made her Vows on her deathbed and was justly regarded as a Saint.

Spiritual writers tell us that sufferings endured and actions performed solely for God are never fruitless. Sooner or later comes the recompense for struggles and combats. The more numerous, the more painful, the more difficult the sacrifices, the more abundant and precious will be the consolation. Rich, indeed, must have been the reward merited by this patient, struggling Community at St. Mary's, especially by Rev. Mother Teresa, who, in addition to all the cares of providing for her little religious family in the face of sickness and of death, had been obliged by circumstances to apply herself to the spiritual formation of the Novices and young members. St. Gregory says, "it is as easy for God to deliver us from great difficulties as from small ones, and more glorious to Him." St. Peter was as safe walking on the water by command of his Master as he was on dry land. But when he began to fear, he began to sink. So Reverend Mother Teresa must have felt that if God had appointed her to govern He would assist her. One of the greatest favours God conferred on the Community in its earlier stages was, giving them for Chaplains holy men devoted to their spiritual and temporal interests. A most worthy successor to Rev. Fathers Paré and Harkin was Very Rev. Father Tellier, S.J., Vicar General of the Diocese. Notwithstanding the many responsible duties and anxious cares which weighed upon this good Priest, he always attended with the

most scrupulous exactness to the spiritual wants of
the Nuns, though in doing so he suffered much inconvenience, and even at times risked his health or life.
In the dark winter mornings he walked a mile daily
through the depths of Canadian snow to celebrate
Mass in the Convent, and, on the day fixed for Confession, he frequently arrived as early as 5.30 a.m.
lest something might occur in the course of the day to
prevent him from fulfilling his duty as Confessor. On
one such occasion, when he reached the Convent,
covered with snow, and almost frozen with the intense
cold, he playfully remarked to the Portress that "none
but dogs and Chaplains would venture out in such
weather." This good Father greatly assisted the
Nuns in temporal matters also, by his wise counsel
and cheering words at times when they might be
tempted to be gloomy or despondent. Needless to say,
how fully Rev. Mother appreciated his kindly ministrations, looking on him as the agent whom God had
sent to her aid to form the interior life in the souls
entrusted to her. In her exhortations to the Religious
she said, "Who are those who find the Institute a ter-
restrial Paradise? Those who have the true interior
spirit find therein a hidden manna. Our aim should
be to lead children to God." And indeed so these first
Religious seem to have done. One of their pupils,
Mrs. Burns, in after years, who, living within the
shadow of Loretto Abbey, had given her two
daughters to God in religion, when asked "Who was
her teacher and what she remembered of her," replied,
"I can recall no Mistress better than Sister M. Joachim.
She prepared me for my First Holy Communion and

I have never forgotten her instructions, but we regarded all these first Religious as saints."

But Rev. Mother Teresa, while forming her spiritual children to the likeness of their Divine Model, was not unmindful of other calls upon her zeal, for in the midst of pressing and responsible duties, she received a request from Rev. Father Ryan, pastor of Brantford, to send Nuns to open a house there. Accordingly on the 17th of August, 1853, the first mission was sent out from Toronto, which took four members from the little group in Bathurst Street. These were Sr. M. Joachim Murray, Superior, Sr. M. Ignatia Lynn, mentioned before, and Sr. M. Stanislaus Hennigan, who had entered soon after Sr. M. Teresa Corrigan. These three were to manage the schools, while the Lay Sister, Sr. M. of the Dolours O'Connor, who had entered in May, 1851, and had made her profession the preceding June, made up the quartet. This last good soul was the first Lay Sister to enter in Canada, and the Institute is still perfumed with the aroma of her virtues, for she was a fitting companion to Sister Ita who came from Rathfarnham, an incentive to all who came after her to embrace the holy vocation of Martha. She entered rather late in life, but lived to a ripe old age and many still remember her fidelity to religious observances which was crowned by a beautiful death. The custom of the Institute is, that when a Religious is dying all the members of the Community who are free from duty with the pupils are summoned by the house bell to assemble in the Infirmary to assist the dying with their prayers. Sister Dolours had many weak spells during her illness, and during the last one the Infirmarian had gone to inform the Superior that she thought it was time to have the bell rung. Great was her dismay when on the stairs she heard the bell peal out, and on returning hastily to the sick room, found Sister Dolours crawling back to bed after having rung the bell herself, lest by any delay she should not see her Sisters praying around her. She calmly expired a few minutes after having performed this last observance for herself.

Sister M. Ignatia had entire charge of the Academy, while Sr. M. Stanislaus, then a Novice, taught the Parochial school and music and drawing, when free from duty in her allotted sphere. The good pastor gave up his residence to the Nuns, seeking accommodation for himself on a neighbouring street. Though his house was found to be rather small and inconvenient for a Convent, still pupils flocked there, and Sr. M. Ignatia, after a hard day's work in the school, was often called upon to cook the dinner for a pretty large family. Examples of virtue never pass unnoticed, and in after years the seed of piety sown in the hearts of the pupils of Brantford brought forth good fruit in some choice vocations, as will appear from the correspondence of the Foundress later on.

Nor were the trials of this early mission, so illustrative of the virtue of these first members, altogether lacking the humourous side, for many years after, gay recreations were spent in the hearing and rehearsing of the antics of the historic Brantford goat. It appears that a great friend of the Community was partaking of its hospitality on a memorable occasion, when it was remembered that the Reverend guest only

69

partook of the beverage of which Leo XIII was so fond, goat's milk, but the only one who could extract it from the unwilling animal was Sister M. Dolours, who was quite ill, so to Sister M. Ignatia, who had probably never seen a goat before her Brantford experience, came the formidable order to "milk the goat." It was like any other order of obedience to this fervent young Religious, and so to Sister Dolours she instantly went to learn how she was to accomplish this feat. She was told she was to take bread into the yard and cry out, "Nan, Nan!" when the goat would follow her into the kitchen. Once there, the animal's horn was to be tied with a rope to the handle of the door and then milked. The goat was easily coaxed into the kitchen, as the horned animal seemed to look on the surroundings as quite familiar, but when an attempt was made to restrain her freedom, she proved to the poor Nun that she was more than a match for her in the ancient game of tag which they played round and round the table. At last a kindly Samaritan passing by, came to the rescue, Nan was vanquished and Sr. M. Ignatia had the reward of heroic obedience.

A stranger experience in the new and more commodious house to which they removed, was the baying of a dog in the quiet hours of the night. The first time the Nuns heard the dismal sound they paid little attention to it, but on the occasion of Rev. Mother Teresa's annual visit to the little Community, after a hard day's work they were awakened by the pitiful howling. Mother Joachim, solicitous for Rev. Mother's rest, and fearing that she would be greatly alarmed, lighted a candle and went into her room, where she found her sleeping peacefully. She then called Sister Ita, and together they visited the house from garret to cellar, examining windows and doors, lest some stray dog had entered, since they had no animal of the canine species themselves, but no dog was visible. So mysterious did it all seem that they mentioned it to the Chaplain in the morning, and upon making further inquiries, were told that the house had the name of being haunted on account of a murder having been committed there in the past and that no one before them occupied it long for that reason. It had been blessed before the entrance of the Nuns, but now the solemn blessing of the Church for expelling evil spirits was pronounced and the weird, uncanny barking was heard no more.

CHAPTER VIII

FOUNDATIONS AT LONDON, BELLEVILLE, GUELPH.

NOTHING daunted by the experiences related in a previous chapter, the Nuns pursued the even tenor of their lives with the result that the schools were well patronized, and children of a tender age became boarders, who in after years were much prized members of the Institute. However, as time went on, a much more desirable opening for a mission was offered to Rev. Mother Teresa, where there were better opportunities of advancing the interests of the Institute, and so on the invitation of Very Rev. Dean Kirwan, with the express permission of Dr. de Charbonnel, the Community was transferred from Brantford to London, a rising, prosperous town of about five thousand souls, situated twenty miles north of Lake Erie, in the roughly triangular district between the Lakes. There the new Convent was placed in charge of Mother M. Berchmanns Lalor, whose Aunt had been Novice Mistress in Rathfarnham, and who was a most zealous Religious, pleasing and agreeable in manner, and devoted heart and soul to the interests of the Institute. The schools opened with a good staff, and pupils flocked to the Nuns who showed the greatest esteem for religious practices, and loving veneration for their teachers. Rev. Mother Teresa exercised a good deal of personal supervision over this establishment, staying there a month at a time, and charming everyone by the simplicity and holiness of her life. A strong feature in her exhortations to the Religious there was the stress she laid on their dealings with the children, "The Nuns should see in their pupils the Image of Him for Whom they have left all, and though firm in exacting accurate knowledge of the lessons assigned their young charges, and while they should make these lessons attractive by explanations and all aids in their power to render, still the great lesson to be implanted in their souls was the presence within and around them of the God Whom they were to know and love and serve for all eternity." She was never weary of telling the Nuns in her own modest way that in teaching science, or history, or music, or art, they might possibly be surpassed by secular teachers who had so many human aids, but in the care of the immortal souls of the pupils they should not allow themselves to be outdone by anyone in the race whose goal was Heaven. Nor indeed did she ever dream of allowing her Community to be satisfied with the idea that they could rest on their laurels as instructresses who had won the highest reputation for teaching. No, she required that they were ever to study better methods in imparting knowledge, and their work was to be so thoroughly prepared that all the knotty problems were to be solved before they reached class. Then fairly equipped with the necessary knowledge they were to pray for light to impart it. She was heard to say, "We need great recollectedness when going to Holy Communion, but even greater, if possible, when going to the children. In Holy Communion we have only ourselves to attend to, but when we are with the children, it is our duty to lead those little ones to Jesus by our example. We are but passive instruments in the hands of God to lead them to Him. Our work is the most divine of all divine works. Our constant aspiration in going to the school should be, 'Incline unto mine aid, O God; O Lord make haste to help me.' One of the characteristics of a good teacher is reverence for the children. We must reverence them for they are the children of God. If we were charged with the care of the children of a King or Queen, how careful we would be how we should respect them. The children we have to teach are the children of the King of Kings. They are holy, for their bodies are the temples of the Holy Ghost. Christ died for them; it is for them that Churches are built, Priests ordained, Bishops consecrated, schools established and Convents founded, particularly ours. Our Rule has for its end the salvation of souls, for this we became Religious—to draw souls to God,— What a sublime office! What great saints to do so holy a work for the All Holy God." She regularly visited the classes and when on the missions, and free from some of the duties which necessarily pertain to the Mother House, she loved to be with the Mistresses in the class rooms. She sometimes brought some light work with her, but her attention to the pupils' manner of answering, their deportment in every detail never ceased. Her presence on these rare occasions was thoroughly appreciated by the pupils, who probably took their cue from the teachers, and there are those now grown old in religion who remember the enthusiasm that was felt when she presided at some class exhibitions in the London mission. But even there trials awaited her.

About 1856 Toronto was divided into three dioceses and the Bulls were received from Rome establishing the two new Sees of Hamilton and London. The Rt. Rev. John Farrell was consecrated Bishop of Hamilton on May 11th, 1856, by Mgr. de Charbonnel, and the Rt. Rev. Peter Adolphe Pinsonneault was consecrated at Montreal on the eighteenth day of the same month, Bishop of London. On the arrival of the Nuns in London, the Very Rev. Dean Kirwan had made over to them the Parochial residence, and this proceeding was displeasing to the newly appointed Bishop, who it was thought, had intended it for his Episcopal residence. The feeling gradually grew upon the Nuns that this act in which they unwittingly concurred was to result in their severance from the Forest City, and the people who had shown themselves so appreciative of their ministrations. Nor did they have to wait long for the confirmation of their suspicions, for ere many moons waned they humbly submitted to authority and abandoned the thought of the fruits of the mission when everything seemed to be in full bloom. His Lordship, Bishop Pinsonneault, ten years after their departure, after a rather stormy administration, resigned his See, having previously removed it from London to Sandwich. How deeply Rev. Mother Teresa felt the abandonment of this new field may be gleaned from her communication with the Superior of the house, in which the lessons of humility and charity which she always inculcated, are fairly set forth.

REV. MOTHER TERESA DEASE

My Dear M. Berchmanns,—

You must wonder at not having a letter from me before this, but I really had not time to write till now.

I saw the Bishop twice since my return. He has no other idea than that you leave London as soon as the will of Dr. Pinsonneault shall be made known to you. I will not say how soon that may be. The united prayers and good works of all our members are now especially called for, in order to propitiate the Almighty that He may give us light, as to what course we are to take for the future. I do not mean with regard to London but to Canada. I wish the Sisters, if health permit, to fast on the eve of St. Anthony of Padua, and to offer their Novena in honour of that Saint for my intention, together with their Communion on the Feast. You all require superhauman prudence and discretion; believe me, one slighting word against the Bishop will not tend to the glory of God, or further your interests with Him. I might naturally judge, referring to our antecedents in Ireland, that anything of the kind could not occur; did I not know from experience that some Sisters in London have not been as silent in His Lordship's regard as they should have been when they did not feel called on or inclined to approve of what he had done? Patience, humility and confidence in God's Will do much more to further our ends than useless talking, for I do believe that there is a treasure of grace and future prosperity hidden beneath our present ignominy if we only merit to reach it by our virtue.

I hope Mr. Kirwan and Kate are well. From what

NEW FOUNDATIONS

I hear I am led to apprehend our kind and best friend
will be deeply involved by this London affair; this
thought in itself is most painful, but it is embittered
by the reflection that we are the reluctant cause. I
shall write soon again, at least as soon as I have anything worth communicating. Love to all.

Yours in C.J.,

M. J. TERESA.

As related before, after the departure of the Nuns,
the Episcopal See was removed from London to
Sandwich, and in ten years from their leaving, His
Lordship, Dr. Pinsonneault, resigned his Pastorate,
and no one felt more happy than Rev. Mother Teresa
to think that her spiritual daughters had not been
in any way accessory to this turn of affairs. Her reverence was so great that in her humility, always examining her own conduct first to see if any possible blame
could be attached to her or hers, that her acquittal of
all culpability in any matter was deemed the most
striking proof of the entire freedom from fault of
the Community. Much has been said and written of
the devotedness of the London people to the Institute
of the B. V. M., but perhaps the best test of the sincerity of their appreciation lies in the fact that the
children whom the Religious had been so successful
in training for a short time, by the express wish of
their parents followed them to their new field of
labour, and in time became members of the Institute
which had satisfied their highest ideals. These first
Religious Founders of the London mission had on
their side such a lively gratitude for the kindness

shown them by the citizens of London that they diffused a spirit of kindly remembrance of this mission among their Sisters which has not yet died out. But God is never unmindful of His own, and although the fruit planted in one garden is not always gathered by the planter, still there are other gardens awaiting the earnest labourers which are ready to yield fruit in abundance

When Bishop Farrell, of happy memory, took charge of the Diocese of Hamilton, he invited the London Community to found a house in Guelph. Here the Religious were most kindly received by Rev. Y. Holzer, S.J., who had the most sanguine expectations of the good to be effected in the royal city of the future, by the presence of the Loretto Nuns, and without flattery it might be said that the results surpassed his most rosy anticipations, for under the patronage of the Immaculate Conception on which feast the House was formally opened on the tenth of June, 1856, the title, "God's little garden," might safely be given to the mission which has produced such flowers for the sanctuary of religion and the adornment of the Institute. The Jesuits, known to be such skilfull cultivators of the Lord's vineyard, had been labouring there for some years before the advent of the Nuns, and the good seed had been sown and only awaited the ministering of tender hands to garner the ripe harvest in a place whose very name would suggest anything but Catholic associations. The city of Guelph was founded by Mr. John Galt, commissioner of the Canada Company, who commemorated the selection of the site with befitting ceremony. On

NEW FOUNDATIONS

April 23rd, 1827, Bishop McDonald of Kingston, commenced the visitation of his immense diocese the same year, and on reaching Guelph was pleased to meet his old friend, Mr. Galt, whom he had not seen since his visit to England in 1823. The Bishop remained several days the guest of the commissioner, who in recognition of the Prelate's services in the formation of the Canada Company, presented him a block of land on a commanding site, overlooking the settlement, on which to erect a Church. He did more; he set men to work to make a clearance through the forest extending from the bank of the River Speed to the summit of the hill on which the future Church was to be erected, and in two hours and ten minutes the avenue which still bears the Bishop's name was opened. On the crest of the hill a large elm tree was left standing in the midst of the clearing, a very prominent feature of the landscape. On the exact site of this tree the present magnificent Church of Our Lady of the Immaculate Conception in charge of the Jesuit Fathers now stands, and opposite is the stone structure built by the pioneer Fathers of the mission for a Convent for the Nuns who were to aid them in their work for the glory of God. Here then came the little colony from London welcomed alike by clergy and laity, and here indeed the fields were white for the harvest.

The generosity of the Catholics of Guelph at this time is gratefully commemorated in the annals of Loretto, and doubtless was a result of the deep abiding faith that procured such blessings for their children. The atmosphere of the Holy Hill, as Guelph is always

79

styled in the Community, had a most cheering effect on the members of the then struggling little band that had gone forth to conquer for Christ. Rev. Mother Teresa had appointed Mother Berchmanns Lalor Superior of the house, and with her were Sister M. Ignatia of Brantford experiences, Sr. M. Stanislaus Hennigan and Sister Ita, the lay Sister from Rathfarnham who was a model of every virtue, filling the offices of cook, infirmarian, portress and dairy maid at the same time with a right good will and a tender solicitude for the well being of all. The house prepared for the reception of the Nuns was scarcely finished when they arrived; the same structure still stands but numerous additions have been made to it, and the Convent of the Royal City has not lost any of its early charm. For charm it must have had after the trying experiences of Brantford and the disappointments of London. The good Father Holzer, S.J., who had been instrumental in bringing them to Guelph, had already a school in pretty fair order conducted by a pious secular lady, and there was prospect of a good boarding and day school at the convent. This worthy Jesuit was a priest well calculated to advance the interests of the Community—the people had the greatest reverence for him, and he in turn had unbounded influence over them. The very consciousness of having such a powerful friend was in itself calculated to give the confidence that secures success.

A very good teacher entered the Novitiate shortly after the foundation in Guelph, Sr. Thomas Murciana, and as she was not physically strong she was sent to the new mission to recruit. Her zeal, energy and industry proved very beneficial to the schools, and indeed to the Novices, whom she taught as well as the pupils. In less than three years from that auspicious tenth of June, 1856, the little Community had increased to thirteen, and the boarding school had an enrollment of forty-seven pupils. Many of these first pupils had such an ardent desire to become Religious, that in less than ten years thirty-four of them assumed the religious habit and became members of the Institute, among the very first being Sr. M. Patricia O'Dea, Sr. M. Regis Harris, Sr. M. Dosithea Gibney, Sr. M. Berchmanns. An amusing incident of what seems to have been an easy transit from the home to the Novitiate in those days was told by the heroine herelf, Mother M. Dosithea, to a large Novitiate over which she presided in after years with unqualified success. One morning, after having previously signified her desire to become a Religious to one of the Nuns, she arrived at school breathless, having walked at a very brisk pace lest she should be late, and rather reluctantly stopped to speak to a Nun who called her aside. The first words addressed to her were, "Frances, would you like to see the Bishop?" "Oh, yes," she replied, for she knew the Community would number one member more if he gave permission for her admittance into it at her very early age. She had an inspiration too, that the result would be favourable, for she was grown beyond her years. She was not disappointed. The Nun afterwards calmly informed her that His Lordship had given leave to have her admitted at once to the Novitiate. Great was her joy

81

6 T.D.

when she returned home and greeted her fond parent with "Oh, Mamma, I can enter this very day if you only give me permission!" The mother pondered and said, "The Will of God, my child, I shall have you ready as soon as possible." That evening found the youthful pupil in the Chapel making her Act of Consecration and renouncing a world she had scarcely known, but with one speck of cloud in the horizon. The Novice Mistress asked her if she had everything she required, when she replied she had all she desired, but a little Indian work basket which she had forgotten and which she could find in a moment if she could run home to get it. The Mistress paused at the unusual request but said she might go. Great was the surprise of her mother, who on seeing her approach their home, went out to meet her and asked her if she had tired of religious life so soon. Hearing what was the object of her coming the mother could not refrain from laughing at the simplicity of the child who reminded her of the day she had received this gift from the Indians after she had proffered them the hospitality of the house as a means of conciliation as she greatly feared the Redskins. Her mother returned with her to the Convent the same evening from what she styled her last visit home.

Instances innumerable of the heroic virtue of these first children of the Institute in Canada are on record, and though some of these early members still survive, many have gone to their eternal reward. It were invidious to select examples of holy, heroic souls from among them, but as in all foundations a few among them seem to have made a lasting impression. One instance may be cited. Sr. M. Vincent Dwyer, a very beautiful young girl in the heyday of youth and spirits, entered the Novitiate in Toronto, and as was the custom in those pioneer days, while receiving her own spiritual training, was set to work to teach music in which she was proficient to some of the pupils. Heart and soul she devoted herself to her allotted task, but after some short space of time Rev. Mother Teresa's watchful eye noted a hectic flush on her cheeks which did not seem to promise length of days. But no complaint came from the fair young soul who would not have deemed the shortening of her life a disappointment; but one thing only she dreaded, and that was to return to the world. This trial Almighty God was pleased to send her. With the hope that her native air might prove beneficial she was sent to the Guelph Convent where every means to insure complete recovery failed to secure for her the boon of health. Her family, anxious to prolong her life even for a time, insisted on taking her home. On her journey thither she was most observant of the monastic rule of silence, and her companion had to testify to her spirit of mortification—that she tried to sit upright, unsupported, although she was then in the last extremity of weakness. On her home arrival she divested herself of the holy Habit, as one might prepare one's head for the executioner's axe, and in her home life followed, as nearly as possible, the observances of the religious life, even to the answering of the Convent bell for spiritual exercises which she heard through the open window in her childhood home. Her death, soon after, far from deterring others from entering seemed to have the effect of increasing vocations to the Institute.

For many years the stream of vocations continued to flow to the Institute, and in the early seventies Guelph was looked on by the Community as the main source of all that was good and beautiful. Its prosperity has continued as the years have gone by, but the Novitiate has had in more recent years many other members from near and distant lands. The Jesuits have ever been the friends of the Institute there, and have always promoted love of learning among the pupils which has resulted in the splendid record of the schools immediately under their charge. In the nineties of the last century the most popular of the later day rhymes which some witty religious composed was "The Guelph Separate Schools." In these schools Rev. Mother Teresa took a deep interest, and their success was a matter of rejoicing to her. The names of Fathers George Kenny, S.J., William Doherty, S.J., and James O'Loan, S.J., took the place of veneration held by Fathers Holzer and Hamel, S.J., and instead of one separate school three flourishing institutions now crown the summit of the Holy Hill. The Convent of Our Lady of the Immaculate Conception has celebrated the golden cycle of its years, and the orator of the celebration in the beautiful Church of Our Lady, Rev. John Coffey, S.J., was generous in his praise of the work done by the Community. No one could speak with more certainty on the subject than the Reverend Father who had grown up in the Royal City and had still his boyish memories with him of the growing Institution. Later, when a prominent lawyer in his native town, before he entered the Society of Jesus, he was able to appreciate the true culture of the Religious training obtained in the schools. In his reference to these early days the speaker was moved almost to tears, remembering the associations of his parents and many of the pioneers of Guelph then deceased, with the early days of the Academy. The Church was filled to its utmost, and many were the blessings invoked on the head of him whose discourse was so uplifting, and who was so fully in sympathy with a subject so dear to the hearts of his hearers. For was not the Academy the Alma Mater not only of his own sisters, but of many of the daughters of those present who had so willingly relinquished all for Christ.

A Reception was held at the Convent in the afternoon of the Anniversary Festive Day, and many were the tributes of praise bestowed on the members of the first Community who had planted the seed which had borne the fruits of such an abundant harvest.

Perhaps the most praiseworthy feature of this mission in those days was the foundation of the night school by Father Plaunt, presided over by M. M. Agatha where classes were formed in the Convent to teach the catechism to the poor who could not attend during the day, and to whom the acquisition of a little knowledge of writing, reading and arithmetic proved an extra inducement. Christmas trees and medals for rewards were also employed as aids to encouragement with most gratifying results, for conversions of whole families in some cases followed in others of individuals. One in particular may be mentioned. A little pupil who had attended this night school was stricken with diphtheria, and as it transpired, while yet a Protestant had contributed eighty Hail Marys to a Spiritual Bouquet for the Father Founder's feast, lying in bed beside her mother, also suffering from the same disease in their squalid home, consigned her little being to the good mercy of God as she had no hope of receiving the Sacrament of Baptism which she desired. When the kindly priest missed the little waif from night school he was informed of her state by the Sister in charge, and immediately went to her home and administered the Sacrament under the adverse circumstances which have been described. When asked by one of the Religious where the new Christian was to be buried, he replied, "What difference does it make? Her soul is in Heaven."

Perhaps nothing gave more pleasure to Rev. Mother Teresa on one of her visits to Guelph than the sight of sixty or seventy of these neglected children of all denominations gathered in the evening in the large day school, and gratuitously taught by the exemplary Miss McElderry, assisted by Mrs. Kelly and Miss Wilson. To these pious secular ladies it was indeed a labour of love for the Master to assist their former teachers in this work of mercy. Nor were the pupils of the boarding school wanting in works of zeal and charity; for gleaning from the Guelph annals the usual closing exercises were not held on a certain year, because the young ladies requested to give a public concert for the benefit of the new church of the Immaculate Conception then in course of construction. It was their idea to give something of their very own—their talents,—to the edifice erected in Our Lady's Name. Their generous efforts were crowned with success, and the singing of the pupils was never heard to better advantage than when with hearfelt joy they used their youthful voices to promote the glory of God and the honour of His Immaculate Mother.

CHAPTER IX

THE CALL TO KINGSTON. A REMARKABLE
VOCATION.   WITHDRAWAL   OF   THE
NUN'S LETTER TO AN ASPIRANT.

THE flourishing condition of the Guelph mission
induced Rev. Mother Teresa to lend a willing ear
to the invitation of the Bishop of Kingston, to found
a branch of the Institute in his diocese, and accordingly with her usual humility and prayerful confidence
she wrote to Dr. Phelan on the 15th of February,
1857:

LORETTO HOUSE,
TORONTO.

Honoured Lord,—

I received your note late on the fourteenth instant,
and beg to say in reply that we are all pleased at the
prospect of being at some future time under your
benign and fatherly patronage, but at the present
moment we are unprepared.   However,—we have
received applications for admission from some very
pious and accomplished persons, whom we hope very
soon to receive; these after a little time can take the
places of our present teachers, who would be happy
with the consent of our good and zealous Bishop to
render service to Your Lordship's diocese.

Our Bishop is expected home in two months, and
Your Lordship's proposal will be among the first
things I shall submit to his consideration after his
return.

88

THE CALL TO KINGSTON

Our number increases but slowly, but those we have, are generally speaking very good. I sincerely trust in God that should we be so fortunate as to come under your holy jurisdiction, we would labour efficiently in carrying out your views for the glory of God and the good of souls. I most humbly recommend myself and the Communities of Toronto and Guelph to Your Lordship's pious prayers.

I have the honour to remain,
> My Lord,
>> Your humble servant,

>>> TERESA DEASE.

The putting forth a branch seemed to indicate vitality in the parent stem, and so Rev. Mother Teresa lost no time in informing the Kingston Prelate of her ability to comply with his request to establish a foundation in Belleville, as may be gleaned from the following:

LORETTO, TORONTO, 17th April, 1857.

Esteemed and Honoured Lord,—

I am anxious to inform you that we can immediately spare some Sisters for your mission in Belleville. Most gladly shall we lend our best efforts to co-operate with Your Lordship for the education of the flock you may confide to our care, provided we obtain the consent of our good Bishop, to whom I intend to write next week. I have no fear that His Lordship will have the least objection to our founding a branch of our Institute in your diocese.

REV. MOTHER TERESA DEASE

Most sincerely wishing Your Lordship all graces and blessings of this holy season and requesting a remembrance in your pious prayers.

I have the honour to remain,
My Lord,
Your obedient servant in J. C.,

MARY TERESA DEASE.

RT. REV. DR. PHELAN,
Bishop of Carrha,
Adm. Apostolic.

Looking over the dates of the last two letters we find that the Foundress did not let the time that seemed propitious fly idly past, but commenced preparations for a new mission in 1857. With Mother Joseph McNamara as Superior, a number of Nuns opened the first house in Belleville at the pressing invitation of the Bishop of Kingston and the Pastor, Rev. Father Brennan. This Loretto was placed under the patronage of St. Joseph, and formally opened on the 20th of August the same year. Belleville, as its name indicates, is a beautiful city on the shores of the Bay of Quinté, and many of the inhabitants had all that went with what was thought considerable affluence in those days. The Academy and schools were largely patronized by the best Catholic as well as Protestant families of the place, and between the Religious and their pupils a mutual understanding and friendship easily obtained. Rev. Mother Teresa

90

remarked the kindly feeling that existed towards her little colony that seemed to prosper from the very first, and at this date it is rather difficult to decide why she thought well to withdraw them in 1865 after a very short sojourn. But brief as was the period of this short lived mission it resulted in some very remarkable vocations, and some of the Superiors who were closest to the Rev. Mother during life, recalled fondly the first dawn of vocation in Belleville.

During one of her visits to this new filiation an unusually heavy snow storm took place, and the Convent door bell was rung by a young lady who asked to be admitted until the storm had spent itself. Rev. Mother happened to be passing through the hall when the young lady entered, and struck by her appearance, invited her into the parlour and opened a conversation with her. The young lady remarked that although her family were living in Belleville she had not known of the arrival of the Religious as she had been away in Kingston for several months, until she made the discovery in this rather peculiar manner. Encouraged by Rev. Mother Teresa she told her that during a visit to Kingston, she became seriously ill and had been advised to return home immediately as she showed symptoms of fever. She rapidly grew worse and her life was despaired of, so that she was gently borne on a stretcher from the station to her home, and during her last conscious moments made a promise that if she ever recovered she would devote her life to God in some religious house. When she became convalescent she distinctly remembered the

91

promise she had made, and this was her first outing since her return home. Rev. Mother was of the opinion that the young girl's visit to the Convent was providential, and other visits followed with the result that the Convent which the young lady had entered by mere accident was the one which she chose for the fulfilment of her promise; although at the time she made the sacrifice of her life she did not know that there was a Convent in Belleville.

Some months after this incident the society of her native town was greatly surprised by the announcement that Mrs. Grant's eldest daughter had entered Loretto Abbey, Toronto. She became in religion Sr. M. Benedicta, and filled important positions in the Institute, the last being the office of Superior in the Belleville Convent. Every talent that she possessed, was from the very first employed in the service of God, and her prayerful, earnest life attracted some rare souls to His love in religion. But it was not alone the Religious, who in a measure, after God, owed their vocation to the advent of the Nuns, that appreciated the benefits of the foundation, for the first pupils of this mission who had remained in the world and married, sent their children to be educated in Loretto Abbey and in other Lorettos when the Nuns were temporarily withdrawn. It is not easy now to understand when everything in connection with the new filiation seemed so satisfactory the reason of their leaving that promising sphere, but the fact is that in 1865 Rev. Mother Teresa again wrote to the Prelate and the pastor that she was about to recall the Nuns from Belleville. On June 26th, 1865, she writes from Toronto.:

Honoured Lord,—

You will hear without surprise that we have come to the determination of resigning the Belleville mission. Please, my Lord, to accept our thanks for the promptitude and kindness with which you afforded our Sisters the services of a clergyman, when they applied for one to Your Lordship.

Recommending myself and our Communities to Your Lordship's pious prayers, I remain,

My Lord,
Your obedient servant in J. C.,

M. TERESA DEASE.

RT. REV. DR. HORAN,
Bishop of Kingston, C. W.

The letter to Rev. Father Brennan, though evidently written with deep feeling, is scarcely more explicit and reads as follows:

LORETTO CONVENT, BOND ST.,
TORONTO, 26th June, 1865.

Reverend and Dear Father,—

I must commence this communication by thanking you for your unvarying kindness towards our Sisters from their first foundation in Belleville to the present time.

This kindness and other circumstances make me feel exceedingly the necessity that forces their removal, on

REV. MOTHER TERESA DEASE

which the members who form the Council of the Community, have decided. You may remember, Reverend Father, that some time ago the same measure had been resolved on and was only deferred, not abandoned. The pain I feel at removing the Nuns is much diminished by the consideration that you will find no difficulty in getting others who will do fully as well as they have done, and perhaps better.

My deep respect for yourself, Reverend and dear Father, makes me cherish the hope that the removal of the Nuns from Belleville, will not cause us to forfeit a friendship we prize so highly as yours, for in the sincerity of my heart I can affirm there are few on whose esteem I would more unwillingly relinquish my hold, than on that of Father Brennan. With the deepest respect, I remain,

Reverend and dear Father,

Your ever grateful servant in C. J.,

M. TERESA DEASE.

It has been stated that the Belleville pupils of this time and as the years went by, did not sever their connection with the Loretto Nuns, and so in 1876 at the earnest request of Monsignor Farrelly, who pleaded that Loretto had never been forgotten by his parishioners. Rev. Mother Teresa sent another band of devoted Religious to the somewhat familiar town of former experience. Loretto, Niagara Falls, and Loretto, Hamilton, had in the meantime been founded, and were so flourishing that the second foundation in Belleville was aided rather than impeded by their existence.

94

THE CALL TO KINGSTON

Before treating of them it may be of interest to follow the closing chapters of the history of Belleville Loretto. Mother Ignatia Lynn was the Superior of the second colony which was warmly welcomed by Monsignor Farrelly; and the former friends of the Nuns who could not do enough to testify their gratitude to, and appreciation of, the much loved Community. The residence of the Monsignor was placed at the Nuns' disposal until the Convent then being built was completed, as the good Pastor wished his schools to open in September at the same time as the opening of the Public schools. But in the case of the select school this was impossible until the Convent was finished. The Separate School opened, however, with a large encouraging attendance and Catholics and non-Catholics who were to attend the Academy waited patiently until the Convent opened its doors to receive them in October. Nothing could have given Rev. Mother Teresa more pleasure than this generous remembrance of the former teachers, and in her visits there her delight was manifest at meeting the children or younger sisters of former pupils who had been so loyal to their Alma Mater. Indeed, she lost no time in visiting this field of promise for the salvation of souls, and aided in a thousand little ways the Nuns' efforts to maintain a school in the old quarters. The Academy was soon filled, but as the house was rather small only a limited number of boarders could be received. These were remarkably fine children and again the heart of the Foundress was consoled by the good reports of them sent by their Mistresses. The years went on and the good work kept pace with the times.

Encouraged by the attendance at Loretto, Belleville, Rev. Mother Teresa felt that something should be done to accommodate the ever increasing number of children, and on one of her visits she noticed a rather attractive and comfortable looking residence with a pretty garden in front of it, and immediately decided to enquire if it might be rented. This she thought would be a cosy and a suitable residence for a number of the Nuns, and at the same time would relieve the overcrowding of the Convent. A certain number of the Nuns might remain to preside over the Students in the Convent, but the new house was to be the real residence of the Community. This house was connected with the Convent by a tunnel, and as this underground passage was by no means an inviting place in the cold Canadian winter, the Nuns who had to pass through it many times during the day often suffered much from cold. One thing was clear to the next Rev. Mother, and that was that a change had to be made, and when new parochial schools were about to be opened in Toronto she deemed it best to call her children home, and use their talents for the benefit of those pupils who were all of the household of the Faith. So much to the regret of ecclesiastical and lay authorities and of parents and children, Loretto, Belleville, ceased to exist, not, however, before this second mission had given its quota of valued members to the Institute. A tie still binds the pleasant town to Loretto Community, for in the Catholic cemetery of Belleville lie the remains of Sr. M. Francesca Sweetnam and Sr. Monica Creighton, Religious noted for deep devotion to the Community and gratitude to God for the inspiration leading them to embrace the Religious life. What was Rev. Mother Teresa's estimate of a Religious vocation may be partly shown by the following letter, but it is to be remarked that while noticing her great appreciation of the call to religion she does not conceal from the aspirant the sufferings which those may expect who voluntarily leave all to follow Christ more closely.

LORETTO CONVENT, BOND ST.,
TORONTO, Feb. 18th, 1874.

My Dearest Lucy,—

I am glad to hear that you are back again in your Convent home. There is much reason to believe that God calls you to Himself in holy religion. You must remember, my dear child, that there are many trials in religious life, and you should therefore pray much and weigh the difficulties that you may expect to meet in the service of Christ, but do not at the same time lose sight of the encouraging truth that God's assisting grace is with those who are really determined to serve Him, making all things possible, if not always easy. It is only the ungenerous that find the duties of Religious life hard; still you must make up your mind that if you do enter, you will have to suffer for Christ. It would be necessary to suffer for Him had you remained in the world and resolved to save your soul, for none attain to salvation but through the Cross. Make trial of your spiritual strength at once. Try to practice humility, obedience and self denial; do

97

not be discouraged at occasional failures in the enterprise, but be sure to rise at once after every fall. You may be sure I shall pray for you, and shall be happy to number you among the members of our holy Institute when the time ordained by God shall have come. I think you had better not enter until you are sure it will not be necessary for you to return home after entrance. You may now consider you have leave to enter. Give my love to all the Nuns. Pray for me and believe me.

Affectionately yours in J. C.,

M. J. Teresa.

CHAPTER X

REV. MOTHER TERESA VISITS IRELAND.
MEETING WITH OLD FRIENDS. HER
RETURN. FIRST VISIT TO NIAGARA
FALLS. QUEBEC VOCATIONS.

IN 1859 Bishop de Charbonnel resigned the See of
Toronto and returned to Europe. He was succeeded
by Bishop Lynch, who was ever the faithful, generous
friend of the Institute. The next year, feeling that
it would be for the benefit of her Community, Rev.
Mother Teresa obtained permission to visit the old
land. An elderly lady, the mother of one of the Nuns,
accompanied her. They arrived in Queenstown after
a passage which does not seem to have been marked by
any remarkable incident, and proceeded by rail to
Fermoy which they reached at dusk. They were
charmed with the wooded, winding avenue that led
to the Convent of Mt. St. John which Rev. Mother
Teresa had never seen before, and of which she had
not heard much, although her sister, Mother M.
Eucharia, was its Foundress. In her letter mailed to
Mrs. Ball in those early days, she says she rarely hears
from her sister but is satisfied to hear good reports of
her. Indeed in those times means of communication
were slow, and the expense of postage to persons who
were poor with the poverty of Christ, an item for
consideration. It would seem then that the beauty of
the King's house, within and without, appealed
strongly to her and that the long years of toil and

separation were in a sense compensated for by the happy meeting of the sisters on the 23rd of April, 1860. During this visit she had not only the happiness of seeing Mother Ball but also Mother Delphina Hart, the Foundress of the Calcutta House. She spent one month in George's Street, the guest of Mother M. Scholastica Somers who was afterwards to succeed Mother Ball at Rathfarnham. This kind Mother had been Superior of the house in George's Street when Sr. M. Teresa Dease received the holy Habit there on the 25th of November, 1845. How affectionate and tender must have been the meeting of these venerated Religious who, widely parted for many years, had worked to extend the reign of Christ in the cold regions of Canada and the tropical country of India as well as in the mild, temperate climate of Ireland. Their conversation must surely have been more of Heaven than of earth, for while their allotted spheres of action were far apart, the end for which they toiled and laboured was the same, and doubtless results were not so widely different. But the time on Mount Thabor was soon spent and the angels of India and Canada were beckoning with no uncertain sign, for on the 21st of June, 1860, Mother Teresa Dease and a religious companion sailed for Canada. They arrived in Quebec on the 4th July where the kind Ursulines gave them a sisterly welcome and having assembled the Community in the parlour, sang the "Laudate." On a former visit to Quebec Mother Teresa was joined by a good pupil of the Ursulines, Mademoiselle Don Carlos, who in Religion took the name of Mary Angela. She is now Mother Angela, and for fifty years has edified the Community by her piety, her unfailing industry and the services she has rendered to the Community in Art which has been her life long pleasure as well as labour. Three of her sisters followed her into Religion, the most convincing proof of the happiness she found therein. On her eightieth birthday, 1916, what she deems a veritable miracle, occurred in her favour. Her sight failing some time previous she was advised to give up painting, but feeling that if her sight was restored she could still do much in art for the glory of God, she made a Novena to the Sacred Heart, and begged the intercession of Rev. Mother Teresa to obtain for her the boon of sight to continue her work. Her letter, recording the grant of her request, and in consequence, her continued practice of her favourite occupation is no less a proof of the potency of the intercession of her former friend, for, written without the aid of spectacles, it is marvellously clear and legible.

On Rev. Mother Teresa's return to Toronto she resumed her duties as Superior, and though physically not very strong, she was ready for teaching on the following September. How untiring must have been her labours in those days may be easily gathered from the fact that her hours in the school were from half past eight to twelve a.m. besides instructing the Novices, reading the public prayers and attending to various household details. In those primitive times, too, the Nuns were not able to secure the services of a Priest to conduct the Annual Retreat, but those first elect of the Institute were so anxious for their spiritual progress that great fruit was gathered from the exhortations and advice given them with such holy zeal by the pious Foundress. Not satisfied with what books written in English pertaining to the ways of the interior spiritual life contained, she made use of the works of French authors that appealed strongly to her spirit of devotion, and translated from the text of the author in his native French into fluent English which came as easily from her lips as though it had been written in the vernacular of those present. But first, last and always she relied principally on prayer, the swiftest, surest mode of communication with God and those who lived with her long years after, can testify how incessant and efficacious was her prayer. But she was a woman of action as well, and one of her favourite themes in the Novitiate was the obedience of a certain young Saint who when asked in what manner he should like to be engaged if death should come to him, replied, "at recreation, for this is the duty prescribed for this hour." In one of her exhortations is found, "Well may we confide in God, for He never wearies in assisting us—we should therefore endeavour with all our strength to be generous with him, and think we have never done enough. Our Rule requires us to choose the worst things; now in wearing an old Habit we suffer no sensible pain, but in toiling to instruct a dull child we really experience pain and suffering. It is wearing on the constitution, it is then we give our life for Christ and He will not be outdone in generosity but reward us a hundredfold." She had had the experience of the suffering and the reward.

When Most Rev. Dr. Lynch succeeded Dr. Charbonnel in Toronto, one of his first cares was for the schools of his diocese, and his fight for the separate schools now flourishing in Ontario may be still remembered by an older generation. Toronto had not then the fully equipped schools of to-day, although Dr. de Charbonnel had commenced the struggle for Catholic education, continued by his successor who had a real thirst for learning for his flock and the zeal that fears no danger. Steadily then he set himself to the task of seeing that each child of his diocese where it was possible should have the benefit of a truly Catholic education. His ideas expressed on all subjects were forcible and convincing, and no one had a keener appreciation of the true and the beautiful. His kindly interest in the Institute ceased only with his life if it then ceased; for it may be hoped that from the heights above he is not altogether unmindful of those over whose spiritual and temporal welfare he exercised the most fatherly care on earth. His horizon was very extended, and even to the far famed Niagara his zeal reached, and so the foundation for which the Nuns had prayed and hoped through his kindly offices was soon to become a reality. The visit which Rev. Mother was ordered to make there for the restoration of her health had made an indelible impression on her and her companion, Sr. M. Antonio, as to the desirability of the site for a foundation, and so after returning home in 1852 she addressed the following letter to the Pastor:

Reverend Dear Sir,—

Were it not that I expected to hear from you every week since I had the pleasure of seeing you in Toronto, I should long since have written to inquire what your intentions are at present with regard to the projected and much desired mission of Niagara. It would give great satisfaction to many here who would wait the invitation of the Master to labour in His vineyard, for here there are some who feel that they stand almost idle.

The return of this season reminds me of that happy time Sr. M. Antonio and I passed under your friendly roof. The good health we now enjoy, the result in a great measure of our visit to Niagara, makes us doubly grateful to God and you. We were disappointed at your not coming to the Reception of Sr. M. Stanislaus and Sr. M. Teresa and hope you will come to Toronto before the season is over. I would gladly send some pictures to my dear young friends and pupils in Niagara, but I must defer that pleasure till I have someone to send them by. Recommending myself to your pious prayers, I remain,

Reverend Sir,

Yours gratefully and respectfully in J. C.,

M. TERESA DEASE.

From the foregoing it would appear that while recruiting her health Rev. Mother Teresa must have been giving instructions to some young people of her acquaintance at Niagara, for no school was established there by the Nuns before 1861, but the health-giving properties of the air of the Falls, she, from her first visit, never doubted. The invitation to labour there was not given until there was practically no one standing idle, for the impetus given by Dr. Lynch to education caused the Toronto schools to be filled with

104

eager, intelligent pupils before he cast his eyes over the Niagara district. Indeed nine years had passed before the projected foundation was made, but Rev. Mother had to practice patience and to wait until many a cloud rolled by, and perhaps it was better so for otherwise her children might not have had the sublime lessons of fortitude and confidence in God which she so strongly inculcated by word and example. On one occasion in those early days she wrote, "I can answer for the true religious spirit of all, they only wish to know the Will of God in order to follow it without hesitation." Well the Will of God was pointing to the promised land.

CHAPTER XI

NIAGARA FALLS FOUNDATION. FIRST
SCHOOL OPENED. FATHER JUHEL. RE-
MARKABLE CONVERSIONS. DIFFICUL-
TIES OF EARLY MISSION.

RETURNING from a visit to Niagara Falls in the
summer of 1861 Bishop Lynch issued a pastoral
letter to his people in which he spoke enthusiastically
of the sublimity of the Falls, the Cataract and River,
and regretted that some great Catholic Institute was
not founded overlooking this wonderful work of God.
"The Cataract of Niagara," he said, "has been called
nature's high altar. The water, as it descends in
white foam, the altar-cloth; the spray, the incense;
the rainbow, the lights on the altar. One must cry
out: 'Great is the Lord, and admirable are His
Works!' How great is Thy Name through the whole
world! Let us adore and love Him with our whole
hearts and our whole souls!" As the pilgrim passes
over one of the bridges that span the islands, he will
see torrents of water rushing madly, as it were, from
the clouds, the only background to be seen; and he is
reminded of the Cataracts of Heaven opened, and the
earth drowned on account of sin. Here the soul
over-awed with terror might exclaim, "Come, let us
hide in the clefts of the rocks, in the wounds of Jesus
Christ, from the Face of an angry God." New
beauties are constantly discovering themselves at

106

NIAGARA FALLS FOUNDATION

Niagara, the eye, wandering from beauty to beauty, compels the soul to salute its Maker. "As always ancient and always new." Before the end of the year the great prelate purchased a tract of land in the immediate neighbourhood of the Canadian Falls. This site, commanding a magnificent view of the upper rapids, the Canadian and American Cataracts, and the river above, was unsurpassed for opportunity of view and unrivalled in its scenic perspective. Six choice acres of this estate the Bishop had surveyed and deeded to the Loretto Community. This princely donation was announced to Rev. Mother Ball by Rev. Mother Teresa.

"I am happy to inform you," she writes, "that our good Bishop has given us six acres of land near the far famed Falls of Niagara. His Lordship wishes to have a Community of regular clergy and another of Nuns there that, as he says, 'the voice of prayer may mingle with the sound of many waters.'" In obedience to the voice and will of the venerated Bishop, Rev. Mother Teresa with one companion, left the city of Toronto on June the sixth by the earliest morning train to Hamilton to meet at the Junction three members of the Community of Loretto, Guelph, whom she called thither to be the first labourers in the new Loretto of the Blessed Sacrament. On reaching Suspension Bridge, they engaged a carriage and pursued their way to the far famed Cataract. On their arrival at the priest's residence they were met by His Grace Archbishop Lynch, and Rev. C. V. Juhel, P. P., who invited them to be his guests for a few days, as

107

the building which had previously been a hotel was not yet in a state of readiness to receive them. During the Sisters' visit at the Pastor's house, a young lady who taught the Public School at the Bridge, called to acquaint the Reverend Father that she was going home for a vacation. Father Juhel expressed regret that the school trustees had no funds to pay her salary, and offered some money of his own as part payment of their indebtedness, which she generously refused, saying she had a comfortable home and would rather do without the stipend than deprive him of any part of his slender resources. God is never outdone in generosity, and the young lady had not long to wait for evidence thereof, for on the fifteenth of August, the same year, the grace of vocation was vouchsafed to her and she returned to the Convent now established at the Falls to offer her services gratis for life as a member of the Institute of the Blessed Virgin Mary, and she proved an efficient aid in the labours undertaken by the first four members. Her golden jubilee, now passed, Mother Aloysius McLaughlin, has not lost the remembrance of those early days although she has laboured most assiduously in other portions of the Lord's vineyard.

After a few days the Nuns took possession of their new home, and in August of the same year two other Nuns arrived from Toronto to carry on the work which the ensuing September was to bring. These two Religious were teachers of music and languages respectively, and great was their desire to meet the requirements of the new school of whose constitution or laws they could scarcely form an idea. In other localities the material prospects are measured by the condition of the inhabitants of the surrounding district, their needs considered and their tastes consulted, but here there were no habitations then in sight, nevertheless with the spiritual end ever in view, the Nuns considered that the whole world comprises God's family and every individual has a soul, so this first band did not stop to analyse where their pupils were to come from, but by prayer and work prepared themselves to do whatever it might please God to allot them in this unique field. Indeed, notwithstanding the beauty of the sight, their trials and privations were neither few nor trivial, as their history will partly show, but they were happy to endure many hardships in labouring to fit the wayside inn for its new purpose; and many were the devices used by the patient Sisters to give a conventual air to their temporary residence. It seems incredible now that to the old frame structure that crowned the dizzy height on the Canadian bluff overlooking the Cataract, large quantities of water had to be brought by the Religious from the river below, a distance of some hundred feet, in a line not diverging much from the vertical. Then, before the purchase of a horse and carriage by the Community, it was not unusual for two Nuns to walk to Clifton village, to buy or provide something for the house, and return home quite exhausted from the fatigue of having travelled over six miles. One of the Religious, Sr. M. Sacred Heart O'Neill, who had some skill as a reinswoman, having frequently driven her father's horses over the Paris roads, turned this accomplishment, as well as every other she possessed, to the benefit of the Community, and her experience in this matter of driving was no small advantage in those pioneer days. A note in the annals records the statement of the Novice Mistress of this Nun that "she gave absolutely all to her Maker," and that she seemed to be the recipient of choicest graces; and children of the pupils of those early days, now in the Novitiate, testify their mothers' reverence for that rare soul. She long sleeps in the little graveyard of the Nuns adjoining the primitive church of Our Lady of Peace, and the two sisters living who followed her into Religion, love to kneel by the little plain cross that marks the resting place of one so active during life in God's service. Fortunately for its purpose of prayer and instruction the Convent still retains its grand isolation, although the means of reaching it now are many—by train or electric car or auto, and a whisper spoken in the telephone office will bring what is required from a long distance in a very short space of time.

Persons who lived in the surrounding district were most urgent in their petition for a Separate school, and so Rev. Mother Teresa assigned the largest room in the house for these children of the growing parish, and this fact was announced from the pulpit the next Sunday by the devoted Pastor to the great delight of all. The Sister who had formerly taught the public school at Suspension Bridge, and had entered the Community in August, was given charge of this first

Separate school at Niagara Falls where she laboured successfully teaching some forty children who walked from Stamford, Clifton, Chippewa, and the vicinity of the Falls, so that the Community was obliged to make many sacrifices in order to erect a school on its grounds near the church. Three or four of the children walked from Sodom, a distance of a few miles, so great was their attachment to their instructress. There were eight or ten Protestants in this primitive school, and their parents could not persuade them to attend the public school, so great was the idea of the advantage they derived from the instructions of this thoroughly qualified Sister. The mounds of snow in winter when there were no electric cars or sidewalks to the convent grounds, were huge, and piled up in impassable drifts in some places; so that during this period the Nuns thought well to close the school for a few days lest the children should attempt to attend and be submerged under the untrodden masses of the beautiful. Their teacher, however, made up for any lapses of time by teaching during the holidays as long as she could obtain permission, and indeed this was on one year nearly the whole vacation, except the time she spent in making the eight days' annual Retreat.

The boarding school opened in September, 1861, and the number of pupils, small at first, soon increased rapidly so that the old frame house could not contain them. Partly through the generosity of the Mother House, a solid stone wing of what is now a stately mansion, was soon erected. Presumedly the pupils of those days were more easily satisfied as to comfort and convenience than their successors now are, and many ladies from the sunny south adorning elegant homes, as well as those mingling in the best society of the most cosmopolitan city in the world, look back with happy remembrance to the primitive days of blissful Niagara. Many years after the foundation a young lady speaking of her life in the Convent of Niagara said, "The Nuns at Niagara Falls were real Nuns, such as you read of in the Lives of the Saints." On being asked why she thought so, she answered, "Because they worked in the fields and did all kinds of manual labour, and seemed so cheerful and happy through all their trials." Indeed the Nuns and pupils of those times were like one family, united in work and prayer. At times they were disturbed at night by travellers seeking admittance, thinking the Convent was still an hotel. The Gypsies often encamped on their grounds, and their appearance caused much anxiety to the Community, without, however, producing any more baneful effect than a very wholesome fear. Sickness, too, visited the early members of the little colony, and it seems strange that the health-restoring ozone of the Falls should not have had a more salutary effect on these pioneers. Probably they were overworked. The record states that there were often five or six in the Infirmary together, and this would mean additional labour for those who had to bear the brunt of the battle and supply for the absent. But God was ever with them, and in incredible ways came to their assistance. The school

LORETTO CONVENT, NIAGARA FALLS.

continued to flourish amid difficulties, and the aesthetic sense of the pupils developed by the presence of the most beautiful scenery in the world which lay out-stretched before their eyes awakened in their souls the love of the All-Beautiful, the Creator. As the climate of sunny Greece and its bright skies are supposed to have affected the minds and spirits of the Hellenes, and made them the happy race they were in historic times, so in the early song of Niagara there is no note of sadness. Indeed, looking over the expanse after many years, eyes are dimmed at the sight which never palls, and the thought of the morning of life here spent which alas passed too soon for those whom the world claimed for its own. But this morning of life so loved by Loretto's children of the Falls, with all its beauty and freshness must have had some clouds and tears, for, in the first years of the foundation their youthful Pastor, full of zeal for souls, and with all the fervour of an Apostle, ere the first harvest had been gathered laid down his spotless life far from his own beloved France. A tablet in the church of Our Lady of Peace records the story of that heroic soul in the scant particulars that mark the existence of every human being—birth, life, death.

He was succeeded in the mission by Very Rev. Dean Mulligan, who was always the faithful friend of the Religious, until his death which occurred in Ireland in 1886. But neither sickness nor the death of friends had the effect of interrupting the work so dear to the heart of the donour, Archbishop Lynch, and perhaps, in no house of the Institute have more

113

marvels of grace been wrought from the very first, than in this Loretto Beautiful. A very remarkable conversion took place during the year 1863. His Lordship, Bishop Farrel of Hamilton, during a visit to Louisville, Kentucky, was consulted by a banker of that city as to a suitable Convent in which he might place his sister to receive her education. His Lordship recommended the newly opened Convent of Niagara, and wrote a letter of introduction to the Superior, which the girl's mother, who accompanied her, presented. Mother and daughter seemed charmed with the Convent and its surroundings, but after the departure of the mother for home the latter seemed somewhat disquieted. On being asked by the Superior the cause, it transpired that in the sleeping room assigned the young lady was a large picture of the Crucifixion which had a very irritating effect on her. She told the lady in charge that, "being a Protestant, and having no faith in images, she did not wish to be saddened by this engraving," and requested to have it removed. The honesty of the young girl in thus revealing what she knew would be displeasing to her newly formed friend greatly impressed the Superior, who saw something good in the displeasing, though honest, avowal. She hastened to conciliate her, and the picture was taken to another room, and in its place was hung one of the Blessed Virgin with the Divine Infant. The young lady then sought an interview with the Superior, and this time thanked her very sincerely for the exchange, admitting that she loved to look on this picture of Jesus and Mary by moonlight, and that it enkindled in her heart not only a love for the Divine Child, but for His Blessed Mother whose intercession she now invoked. Still prejudice dies hard. One Sunday evening as the Priest was on the Altar to give Benediction the Religious in charge of the pupils came to the Superior's prie dieu and told her this young lady had refused to enter the Chapel. As all pupils know before entering the Academy they are to conform externally, and their parents' consent to this regulation, the refusal was looked on as a serious breach of discipline. The young lady was gently but firmly reminded that she had written her consent to obey the prescribed order of the house, and that she was free to return to her family the following day if she refused to comply with the regulations. She went in and when Benediction was concluded and the signal given for the pupils to leave the Chapel, she remained kneeling before the Tabernacle for a long time. On being questioned why she did so, she replied, "As I entered the Chapel the Priest raised the Sacred Host, and I fell on my knees as if pressed down by a Divine Hand. What I felt then I can never express. I went in a vexed and disrespectful Protestant. I am now a Catholic in firm faith, and wish to be baptized by my brother's friend, Rt. Rev. Bishop Farrell."

The members of her family were apprized of her intention and freely gave their consent to her request. She received the necessary instructions, was accompanied to Hamilton by the Superior and was baptized and Confirmed by Bishop Farrell in his Cathedral.

115

She lived ten years after in her home, faithfully discharging her duties as a Catholic, and died surrounded by her Protestant relatives. Her last words were the holy Names of Jesus and Mary, and with her Crucifix and rosary in her hands she breathed her last on the sixteenth July, 1873. Her aged Mother wrote to the Community what her daughter dictated during her last illness, and after her burial sent the account of her last moments. This was perhaps the first of a long list of conversions, not more remarkable than that of a child eleven years of age, who came to the Convent more recently, and besought her mother who had practically abandoned her religion to allow her to be baptized a Catholic, as she had never received the Sacrament of Baptism. After the mother's consent was obtained the child was carefully instructed and prepared for the reception of the cleansing Sacrament, and it must be admitted that this child on whom the regenerating waters of Baptism had never been poured, seemed to have already received it by desire, so great was her thirst for the knowledge of God and the means of salvation. Some there were who came to the Convent not knowing they were Catholics until after having spent some time there, when the beauty of religion began to dawn on them, and when seeking their parents' permission to embrace the tenets of the Catholic Church, they discovered they had been already baptized in that Fold. As in many other Communities, doubtless, some not only received Faith in the Convent but also a Religious vocation as in the case of Sr. M. C. who, having been admitted as a pupil in 1900 and having charmed all her companions by the sweetness and amiability of her disposition, embraced the Faith and almost immediately sought admission to the Novitiate. Her request was not granted until after her graduation, then she renewed her petition with increased ardour, and in the full bloom of her ripening womanhood, remarkable for her grace of form and beauty of feature, she entered the Community where she lived holily for ten years and died a happy death May 12th, 1916. The majority of pupils, of course, remain in the world, and many an edifying letter is received from them by the members of the Community, telling of the victories of Faith in our day.

After the death of Very Rev. Dean Mulligan, Rev. Richard O'Connor, a future Bishop of Peterboro', ministered to the spiritual wants of the mission and Community, and many and kindly are the remembrances of him by the members of the Community in these early days. Then the wonder worker, Fr. McSpirit, came, and the miracles he wrought are still fresh in the memory of those who saw them or heard of them. Indeed few canonized Saints could be accredited with greater healing powers than this humble, holy man, who never accepted the slightest recompense for the incomparable blessing of health he restored to the multitude. The Carmelite Fathers have been in charge of the Falls Parish for over thirty years, and in all that time what lessons of devotion to the Mother of God have they given not only to the pupils, but also to the Religious. No one appreciated

117

these instructions more than Rev. Mother Teresa, and many a time her visit to the Falls was prolonged by the expectation of a good sermon from the future General of his order, Father Pius, or a few words from Father Kreidt on his favourite theme, the love of God. All these instructions sank deeply into her soul, and her beaming countenance gave evidence of the joy she felt when her spiritual yearnings were satisfied. Could she have looked into the future she would indeed have rejoiced to see the number of persons distinguished in Church and State, who from time to time visited this foundation of hers, to witness God's image of eternity from its commanding dome.

CHAPTER XII

ROYAL VISITORS. JUBILEE CELEBRATION.
NEW YORK AND SAN FRANCISCO MEET.
TABLEAU. VIVANT. PROGRESS.

HIS Eminence Cardinal Merry del Val, when Able-gate to Canada, 1897, was informed of the beauty of the site, and accompanied by Rt. Rev. Dr. Dowling and Dr. Treacy witnessed the majesty of God in His handiwork, from every point of vantage, verandah and dome, and bright are the recollections of the few favoured children who were spending the holidays at the Convent who on their own cherished soil had the happiness of receiving the benediction of the future Cardinal, and hearing his generous praise in their own tongue of the unrivalled beauty of their Alma Mater. These recollections of favoured visits so dear to the heart of every school girl, form a large part of the blissful reminiscences of the Alumnae of Loretto of the Blessed Sacrament, and the after-glow of the sunny days, is often in striking contrast to the sombre hue of the rainy period that must come into every individual life. For "into every life some rain must fall, some days must be cold and dark and dreary." Happy those whose Faith has provided them with the sunshine that never fails, the secret indwelling of the spirit of peace,—the love that reached from earth to Heaven. "As the seeding, so will be the harvest," and what seeds of virtue have been faithfully sown in the lives of the young, the flowers of eternity alone can show. **119**

REV. MOTHER TERESA DEASE

When His Majesty, King George V, was in Canada in 1901, the then Duke of Cornwall and the Duchess, and their suite, accompaniel by the Governor-General, Lord Minto, and his suite, visited the Convent, as they were advised by the Hon. Mr. Scott of Ottawa, that the best view of the wonderful Cataract was from the dome of the Convent. When the Royal visitors arrived at the Convent they were received most cordially at the entrance by Archbishop O'Connor, the Superior General, Rev. Mother Ignatia, and the pupils and Religious of Loretto. His Grace, the Archbishop, accompanied by Mgr. McCann, arrived from Toronto the morning of the royal visit to pay his respects to the future King. He was invited to luncheon by His Royal Highness who was surpassed in graciousness only by His Royal Consort, Queen Mary, with whom the Archbishop seemed to be most favourably impressed. The pupils grouped in tiers, opposite the entrance in the large hall, voiced their greeting in song, and three times, at the request of the Royal Visitors, rendered the "Ave Maria Loretto," specially composed for the young ladies of the Academy by the late Hon. T. V. Welsh, former Senator of the United States. The noble appearance of Archbishop O'Connor on that occasion was most favourably commented on, and the great Churchman seemed to be in happiest mood accompanying His Majesty through the halls to the wondrous dome from which the spires of Buffalo, distant about forty miles, could be seen. But the everlasting wonder may be viewed from almost any window in the house, and it were difficult to say whether the scene is more beautiful in the radiant morning when the river from the rapids is silvered up to the horizon, and the glory of a new summer day has dawned, or in the full glare of a midday sun when different rays are reflected from the foamy mass, and the quarter rainbow rests one end on Goat Island, and dies away in the centre of the arch that spans the Cataract; or in the evening, when the half circle of brilliant colouring rests on both banks like a fairy Colossus, under which, however, no boats may pass. The future Sovereign most fittingly commemorated his visit by the granting of a medal annually through the Governor-General of Canada for English Literature.

The celebration of the Eucharistic Congress at Montreal brought visitors from many lands to Canadian shores, and naturally enough the overseas Prelates before leaving the country were anxious to see God's wondrous work in seething, restless Niagara. Again the Convent was favoured by its commanding situation for viewing the sublime scene and the visitors' book records the distinguished names of His Eminence Cardinal Logue of Ireland, and His Grace Archbishop Bourne of England, besides that of His Grace Archbishop Blenk of New Orleans, His Grace Archbishop Gilloa of Mexico, Rev. Bernard Vaughan, S.J., Dr. Burke, and many other distinguished guests.

The same year in the golden October of 1910 His Eminence Cardinal Vanutelli, who represented His Holiness Pope Pius X at the Eucharistic Congress, visited the far famed Falls on his journey homeward. The announcement that the great Prelate had expressed a wish to visit the Convent caused a thrill of expectant joy in the Community, and preparations were made to welcome him within the very walls that had re-echoed the strains of welcome to a King. This was to be the crown of Loretto's honour roll of visitors, and so from Toronto the then Superior General of the Institute, Rev. M. Victorine Harris, journeyed to Loretto, Niagara, and there, with the Religious of the Convent, awaited the arrival of His Eminence. At 12.30 his auto was seen at the Convent gate, and in a few moments the pupils were in their allotted places on the platform of the Concert Hall, expressing their greeting to the representative of the Christ on earth. After replying graciously to the address read by one of the pupils, His Eminence blessed all who were present, and after expressing his appreciation of all he had seen and heard returned to his hotel.

In accordance with the intention of Bishop Lynch that the most sublime work of nature should have the effect of turning the heart from nature to Nature's God. exposition of the Blessed Sacrament is permitted in this house on the first Sunday of each month, and the half hourly adoration of Nuns and pupils is looked forward to with holy pleasure. Protestant pupils are never expected to spend any time in adoration, but it invariably happens that they request to be permitted to pass some time during exposition in the Chapel, and their presence there on these solemn occasions is doubtless the source of untold blessings to them in after life. The most recent event in the history of the Convent was the celebration of the Golden Jubilee at which neither Archbishop Lynch nor Rev. Mother Teresa, the Foundress, was present, but often and reverently were their names mentioned by the members of the Alumnae who held their first general meeting on that occasion. From far and near of the North American Continent they came, and many a fervent prayer was offered up in the overcrowded Chapel by young and old, for those who had been the means of bringing the blessings of faith and love of God into their lives. "Why was not a general meeting of the Alumnae Association held before?" was on the lips of many on that memorable occasion. This question was answered by "Una" (the late Mrs. Austin Ford) in the New York Freeman's Journal. Her answer seems to be the right one, because the graduates of Loretto, Niagara, are all over the land, and do not belong to any particular section of the country. Indeed she might well have said so, for her own children were cherished pupils in the eighties, and she knew the difficulty of bringing New York and San Francisco together, even for a short time. However, loyally and promptly they responded to the invitation to come, and the proverbial excuses were rare. Over two hundred met during the celebration who had at different times been lulled to sleep by the music of the Cataract, and sincere and heartfelt were the greetings exchanged and the pleasure experienced by these representatives in meeting their former Mistresses. The life of the Institution was cleverly portrayed by the nine graduates of the Jubilee year, and no more interested spectators viewed the tableau "Vivant" than their elder sisters, who with the glad and sad experiences of life showered congratulations on the gifted participants.

Photographs of young and old were permitted to be taken; and the treasures conveyed to their homes are doubtless a source of permanent pleasure. The classes of different years were kodaked on many parts of the grounds, and a favourite resort for picture-taking was in the vicinity of Rev. Mother's grave. Rev. S. McDonald, O. C. C., and Rev. Dr. Tracy of Toronto addressed the Alumnae and pupils on the first and second days respectively. In both instances, high ideals were pointed out, memories of the past revived, and the gilded sphere of the influence of women clearly mapped out. Very Rev. Dr. Kidd, the Administrator of the Toronto diocese at the time, was present on the third day. Many hearts were surely brought nearer to God, and early friendships more firmly cemented under the sunny skies that overhung the early years of happy girlhood. From Niagara University came the generous offer of the celebration of fifty Masses by the Reverend Fathers for the welfare of the sister Institution. The British and American flags floated from the dome in friendly rivalry and a rounded cycle of strenuous years was completed.

Very early in the history of the Convent a large day school was opened in Clifton, now styled Niagara Falls, Ontario, some three miles from the Cataract, and this succeeded so well that it was taken under the management of the Separate School Board and the Trustees of the said Board voluntarily raised the salary of the Nuns, to show their appreciation of the work done for their children. Very many Italians attend this school, and a pleasing feature of Cardinal Vanutelli's visit to the Falls, already referred to, was, that when his carriage was passing to the Cataract, these children lined the sidewalks adjacent to their school building and sang their simple songs in his own dear Italian language. God's little ones the world over, possess an attraction all their own, and indeed it might be surmised that hearing his native language not far from the world renowned Cataract, gave to His Eminence a thrill of pleasure. In "The Blindness of Dr. Gray," Cannon Sheehan has immortalized school life at Niagara, and it is no small tribute to his genius to say that he who had never visited the Falls, gave such a perfect picture of the composition of the school and the sentiments of the pupils that it is accepted by every Loretto graduate.

We have dwelt so lovingly on the beauty of the Falls and their environment that we cannot resist the temptation to end this chapter with a quotation from "Niagara and Its Falls," by Audubon, the American naturalist. "After wandering on some of our great lakes for many months I bent my course towards the celebrated Falls of Niagara. When I entered my hotel I saw several views of the Falls hanging on the walls, which so disgusted me that I suddenly came to my better senses." "What!" thought I, "have I, too, come here to mimic Nature in her grandest enterprises, and add my caricature of one of the wonders of the world to those which I here see? No, I give up the vain attempt. I will look on those mighty Cataracts and imprint them where they alone can be represented —on my mind."

125

CHAPTER XIII

FOUNDATION OF LORETTO CONVENT, BOND ST. ACADEMY WELL PATRONIZED. REV. MOTHER TERESA AGAIN VISITS IRELAND IN QUEST OF POSTULANTS, SUCCESS. YOUGHAL. RATHFARNHAM. HOME AGAIN.

THE next foundation after the Falls in the order of time was Loretto Convent, Bond St., Toronto, in 1862. The Convent on Bathurst Street, which had been looked on as such a boon by the early members, soon became entirely inadequate to accommodate the number of pupils, who flocked to the now well established school, and as the number of the Community had also been greatly augmented by the vocations of the last few years, another home had to be sought for the Head House. Then again Archbishop Lynch, whom God had raised up to help the struggling Religious, came forward with his generous, timely aid and advice. He advised the building of a house on Bond Street on ground belonging to the ecclesiastical corporation and gave to the Community a lease of this property for five hundred years. How this school flourished is now a matter of history. At first there were very many Protestant pupils, especially among the boarders, very nice children, who are still fondly remembered by the Nuns, and who were very assiduous in learning all that was then deemed essential to the education of a refined young lady. A good solid

126

house was erected on this property by the Nuns, and again from the annals is gleaned the anxiety and care bestowed on its construction by the gracious donour of the land. The large amount paid for the building was furnished in part by the father of one of the newly entered Nuns, M. Agatha Doherty, who, on the day of her profession, paid over to Rev. Mother Teresa the full amount of her dowry.

For the first four years in Bond St. Rev. Mother Teresa continued to teach the highest English class, as well as French and Italian, but again Providence came to her aid by sending her a postulant fully capable of relieving her altogether of the highest English class. This young lady, Miss Elizabeth McGann, in religion, Sr. M. Eucharia, a brilliant, accomplished girl, and sincerely pious, was a most valuable acquisition to the Community at the time, for her rare musical talent was soon discovered, and from the very first she taught with success. She was the first of a family of educators who joined this branch of the Institute, for four of her sisters followed in her footsteps, and their names are held in benediction by a grateful, rising generation of Religious, who, after the call from God, owe their vocations to these model teachers. But although, as has been noted, Providence invariably came to Rev. Mother Teresa's assistance at the opportune moment, still relief from what was troublesome, disagreeable, or distasteful did not come; for a great feature in the success of the school at the time was the production of little dramas or dialogues as entertainment, and these were rendered in French and Italian as well as in English. Rev. Mother Teresa had then to continue her role of instructress in these little plays which were so much admired, and attended by the best people of the city whose children could not give them greater pleasure than by acquitting themselves creditably on these occasions. Invariably there was a clergyman present of the nationality of the language spoken, who could testify to the correctness of the pronunciation, and the faultlessness of the accent of the speakers, who had copied every tone and gesture of their incomparable teacher. So the Superior, whose mind and thoughts were occupied by much more important subjects, had to be intently engaged in work which she would gladly have resigned to another.

Dr. Lynch was so pleased with the progress of this school, and the good results of the teaching, that he spoke of it in the Cathedral, and among other things said that a young lady's education was not considered finished in Toronto until after she had attended the Convent. Great umbrage was taken at this speech by certain persons, and soon after the number of Protestants greatly decreased, their ministers had obtained for them schools to meet their requirements, but nevertheless a kindly feeling still exists between members of the families who at this time patronized the school, and the Religious who knew them or heard of them from others. Indeed there are men beyond the middle milestone of life who remember when they, as little lads, stood behind the Bishop's chair to see their grown sisters at some entertainment, for in no other part of the hall would they have felt secure from not receiving an invitation from some Religious to withdraw, but there they stood and felt welcome, from a kindly pat on the head or a reassuring nod from the great Prelate, which to them was perfectly intelligible.

The withdrawal of the Protestants did not make any appreciable difference in the number of the pupils, for Catholics almost immediately took their places, and soon it was quite evident that the boarders would have to go somewhere else, for the day scholars alone filled all available space. But success or failure seemed to have no effect on the guiding head that was ever well balanced, and indeed if the Chief Superior's sentiments may be judged, from the letters that went forth to some who had gone out from that privileged Nazareth to labour in other fields, failure with its attendant humiliations was to be embraced as readily as success. To a Sister on a mission she writes:

LORETTO, December 5th.

My Dear Sister N.,—

Aim at being very humble, and God will bless you, and those for whom you labour, and the holy Institute to which you belong. I know well you are not one of those who would consider themselves slighted and belittled by the supposition that they were not quite as enlightened as others, if not more so. God preserve you from this folly—this flying from contempt, which our holy Rule enjoins us to love and embrace after the example of Christ; there is not much danger of our hunting after honour and a great name, but we must hate and abhor the least approach to this. I know perfectly well that you look to the glory of God, which might in some degree be compromised, if blame

129

should happen to fall on the teachers of one school; besides, justice requires that we do our duty efficiently and appear to do it, or at least do not appear not to do it. Love to all.

Yours fondly in C. J.,

M. J. TERESA.

Such was the teaching that emanated from Loretto, Nazareth, and indeed, like the teaching of the Saints, it might suit any time or any place. The large increase of pupils at the Bond St. Academy necessitated an additional supply of teachers, and as new foundations were also in prospect, Rev. Mother Teresa, with her usual foresight, bethought herself of again visiting the Old Land, although at the time no word was spoken of the object of her visit. Her letters at this period give us, perhaps, the best insight into her character, and the habitual expression of her charity, for she never saw an edifying sight or witnessed an act of virtue without recording it. Thus her great solicitude for the members of her own Community, and appreciation of what was good in others, are very marked in this correspondence, and the beauties of God's demesne did not pass unobserved. On her journey she writes:

My Dearest M.M.,—

We got on so far extremely well, thank God, and are now in New York, all very well. We had a charming journey along the Hudson although it was very fatiguing. Dear F. J. is very well, but, like ourselves, tired. I cannot say where we shall be settled during our stay in New York, but I suppose we

130

shall know before I close this letter. I hope you are all well and happy, trying to contribute to the glory of God through holy charity, which is the surest means you could adopt. Father Perrault came to the Sisters of Charity Convent with us and then took us to Manhattanville, where we are now enjoying the edification, hospitality and great beauty of the place. Give my love to all the dear Nuns and Novices, and pray for

Yours fondly in J. C.,

M. J. TERESA.

A little later she writes:

CONVENT OF THE SACRED HEART,
MANHATTANVILLE, N.Y.

My Dearest M.M.,—

We are still in New York, enjoying the hospitality of the good Nuns of the Sacred Heart, by whom we are highly edified. Their piety seems so solid and their views so simple. I think they have only the glory of God in view. Your last letter was really consoling and I feel that the cause of this consolation will continue—Father Jamot said to me, "You may be sure the Nuns will do their best," and I feel it will be so. Everyone understands that there is no fault which is not to be preferred to a breach of charity. M.M.R. has not yet arrived, I believe she has been ill. I hope she may come before we leave to-morrow. Mr. and Mrs. Keogh (Sr. M. Ambrose's father and mother) came to see us last Sunday and seemed extremely well. I am in hopes that Mr. and Mrs. Austin may return before we leave. Give my love to

———— and all the Nuns and Novices. The name of the steamer by which we leave to-morrow is the "Java." You must pray to dear St. Joseph under whose patronage we set out.

Yours fondly in J. C.,

M. J. TERESA.

On the 25th May, 1870, before she put her foot on her native soil, we find her writing to the little flock whom she had left behind, whose anxious prayers followed her over the waters. "We are now nearing land, I mean Queenstown. Deo Gratias. After having passed some days in Liverpool with the good Sisters of Mercy, we expected to have reached here on the twentieth, but were obliged to go on to Liverpool, on account of the dense fog, as they could not see the land or meet a pilot. We have had a good passage, thank God. I am extremely anxious to hear how you all are, especially dear Sister M.M. I shall write at length when I get to land."

Her extreme penetration of character was of the greatest aid to her in her administration, and hence in the next letter dated the sixteenth of June, 1870, this remarkable passage occurs: "I sometimes wonder at the unreasonableness of some who think they are mightily injured if others do not think exactly as they do. They seem to regard that as a sort of persecution." She goes on to advise, "If all would try to prefer others to themselves in wisdom as well as the rest, what a Community we should be. I hope that you and dear M.M. get on happily together. I am sure you both do your best, that God's will may be

132

done, and you will reap the reward of your humility and charity. It makes the success of your Distributions in Canada. Again I repeat what I think unnecessary, because I know you all try to observe the rules of charity, and wish to prefer others to yourselves. I say this in all sincerity." The next letter is dated 24th June, 1870, and runs thus:

LORETTO ABBEY, RATHFARNHAM.

This is the feast of the Sacred Heart, and we have Exposition of the Blessed Sacrament. The church is most beautifully lighted up. I have been at Adoration and have prayed for you all. I had a kind letter from dear Father Jamot, in which he said that he offered Mass at Altars to which a special blessing is attached, and that he did not forget anyone, especially his dear Community of Loretto. He said also that the little he did for the Community was a recreation and not work. What a true and holy friend, what a blessing and privilege to have such. Every new act of kindness makes me think of the money he got for us when we needed it so much, and had so little chance of getting it. I should be sorry that the Nuns would ever be forgetful of his great services. We are extremely edified by all we see. This is really a splendid Community in every respect. The Novices look like so many angels. There are fifty in the Community and Lay Sisters Department. I don't think there is any Community that surpasses this. The Novices have every advantage, they have their own quarters quite separate from the Community, and have everything

133

to lead them to perfection. How sanctifying and beautiful the divine solitude they enjoy here. The Novices might spend their vacation at the Abbey.

With fond love to all, I remain,

Yours fondly in C. J.,

M. J. TERESA.

The next letter comes from Loretto, Youghal, by the sea, and in it her extreme solicitude for the spiritual and temporal well being of the Nuns is manifest. In every letter written from the Old World at this time, one Sister was especially inquired for, and the conclusion that she must have been ill, forces itself upon us, for her tenderness for the sick and aged was sincere and delicate. A Sister who was never very strong and grew old, one would suppose, before her time, wishing to see Rev. Mother, was told she was in the parlour treating with a lady on important business about the school, she with difficulty crept down the stairs and waited to ask some slight permission, until Rev. Mother dismissed her visitor. The time seemed very long, and instead of finding the least fault with her importunity Rev. Mother said very sweetly to her: "This was too much for you, dear M.M. I am so sorry you were kept waiting so long."

A visit of almost two months to her first home in religion must have been a perfect tonic to her, for we find her trying to answer requests from Canada that her letters are too few, by promising that the irregularity in the reception of them by her Toronto children would not happen again. She writes:

134

LORETTO CONVENT, BOND STREET

LORETTO CONVENT,
YOUGHAL, 11th August, 1870.

My Dearest M.M.,—

I cannot understand the complaint that I do not write, except by forming the conclusion, that it is with you as with me, for I think I write very often, and do not receive as many letters as I expect. Now I shall D.V. so arrange that either M. M. Stanislaus (her companion) or I shall write once or twice a week, and note in a memorandum the date of our letters. We left Rathfarnham on Monday the 8th, and intend to leave for Fermoy on Saturday, the 13th D.V. Nothing could equal the kindness of the Nuns in Rathfarnham, and if our visit was not most beneficial it would be very hard to account for it. I am delighted to hear that all things are going on well. Sister M.N. was not at the Retreat in Guelph, but I suppose those who were not in Guelph will make their Retreat in Toronto. We enter Retreat on the 16th of August, D.V. I hope we shall make a good one. The mother of one of our Fermoy Nuns died to-day, will you kindly pray for her. I write in a hurry and am scarcely able, but from your letter I see you consider I am not a very good correspondent, so I determined to answer by return of post which I have often done before since I came. I am glad to hear Sister M.N. is better or at least as well as usual. Did she get my letter? Give my love to all, and believe me.

Yours fondly in J. C.,

M, J. TERESA.

135

REV. MOTHER TERESA DEASE

Her sympathy has been mentioned before, but it was a wider one than one might expect to find in the cloister, and did not altogether confine itself to individuals but was extended to nations. The war cloud was hanging heavily over France at this time, and from her letters we glean not only her own personal feeling for the bleeding country, but the feeling in Ireland which owed so much to France in two Continents. On the 9th September, 1870, she writes from Fermoy Loretto:

My Dearest M.M,.—

In a letter to M. M. Joachim I asked her opinion about our staying in Ireland till May. I mentioned in some letters that I sent the cheque endorsed to M.M., which I sincerely hope she has received before this. Tell dear Sister M.N. I was delighted to get her letter. I cannot tell you how relieved I am to think that good Father Jamot is in Toronto to advise you in your doubts and remove your difficulties. I wrote to him but got no answer, so I did not write again. I hope you all pray for poor France. When we look around at the statues, pictures, and other objects of piety and think that it is to France we owe them, I feel we ought to do something for her, at least by our prayers. Nearly all Sodalities and other institutions of piety took their rise there. The poor Emperor did good though he may have done some evil. God grant that he may now turn to Heaven for help and consolation, since earth has abandoned him. Are we expected to make purchases and pay our way without money? We have very little remaining of what we took from

Guelph, none of it came from Toronto. I think, however, it may be safer not to send money as it might be lost. We can use some of the Postulants' money until we reach home. I am so much pleased to hear such good accounts of the affairs in Toronto, Guelph, Hamilton and the Falls—I feel quite at ease. I hope you have a good prospect of pupils this year. All seem delighted with the Guelph Retreat. I hope that of Toronto was equally satisfactory. Poor M.M.B. is so kind, I think she would like to return to Canada, and that for pure zeal for the glory of God. She loves Canada warmly, as much, or more than ever. I never esteemed her more than I do now. I see her sincere attachment to the missions of Canada. With love to all, I remain,   Yours fondly in J. C.,

M. J. TERESA.

Her eyes were now beginning to turn homeward, or rather missionward, for at the end of her sojourn, the main purpose of her visit is disclosed, although she does not seem to have missed any opportunity of seeing what she thought might prove of benefit to herself or others. Rather conservative in her views, her admiration for what was old and tried was literally unbounded, but this did not in the least prevent her from assimilating what she deemed of worth in the new. She writes again to her assistant in Canada:

LORETTO CONVENT,
FERMOY, 23rd September, 1870.

My Dearest M.M.,—

We have made up our minds to sail D.V. on the

137

7th of October by the "Prussian," the same steamer as the Archbishop went by. We hope by that time to have done nearly all we could do, by remaining a shorter time than May, so that you may in all probability expect us the 23rd or 24th of October. I was anxious to go with B.W. but that was impossible, as by doing so, we would have left much undone. I did not like to leave Ireland without seeing the great and celebrated Ursuline Convent of Blackrock, Cork, as we were in the County. We went there on Wednesday last, and were received and treated in the kindest manner. We were very much pleased with everything. We saw M. M. Gonzaga who wrote all the reflections for the feasts of the year, the month of May, and the Ursuline Lenten Monitor. She is a nice, dear, simple creature. Indeed, it was she who stayed with us for the most part of the time we spent in the Convent. I feel more pleased than I can tell that I paid this visit. I find that we can get the habit cloth and other things as cheap in Canada as in England, so having no money to spare for such purposes, I did not get anything in that way. I am delighted to hear that the Archbishop is well. I am quite sure you were very glad to see him. I feel surprised you did not say a word of Father Jamot. I hope he has arrived safe and well, long before this. I am sorry to hear poor Sister M.'s knee is sore. Sister M.M.M. continues much the same evidently, or at least is little worse than when we left, and this is a great consolation to me.

The musicians of Fermoy decline the honour of accompanying us to Canada, so we have to take a little girl who has great natural talent, and promises to be a fine musician. She has been only two years learning the piano, and has had some tuition on the harp. We bring a Postulant Lay Sister who is a stranger, but much recommended, and she seems to be very good. The people here are in deep sorrow about the poor French. Excuse my spirit of poverty that led me to write you on this scrap of paper. With love to all, I remain,

Yours fondly in C. J.,

M. J. Teresa.

The letter was commenced on a half sheet of green paper and ended in a crossed half sheet of white.

And so again the sea she crossed before had to be measured back and with no faint heart, for she brought with her many substantial gifts of money and art treasures, and a decided increase in the labourers for the wide field, accordingly we find her sailing for home, and have now come to her last letter from the Old Land. What this parting, which she must have realized to be her last, meant for her, it is difficult to say. The final severance from home and kindred, and for both she had the deepest affection naturally, but not a thought of this found expression in words. And so she again addressed her assistant on the 1st of October, 1870.

My Dearest M.M.,—
I wrote to say we would sail on the 7th of October, but that was impossible without making the sacrifice of a nice accomplished Postulant. No one is more anxious for my return than I myself am. I would

have gone cheerfully and joyfully with B.W., but did I go then I should have left undone the most useful part of my mission. We are getting some very good Postulants. We shall, please God, be in Quebec by the end of October with two Lay Sister postulants, three Choir Postulants, probably, and a Professed Nun from Fermoy. I hope this will prove a great blessing, as they are all extremely good. No doubt at all about that. I cannot but admire the generosity of this Community in offering us their best members, had they volunteered to come. I am anxious beyond expression to get back to Canada. I would not remain an hour in Ireland, but with a view to the interests of Canada. I was cheered to hear there was a good prospect for the schools. I think those Sisters we bring will be useful. They are pious and humble, which, if they were nothing else, would make them most useful. I hope in God I shall find all well and happy. If I could have staid till May one of the Postulants could by that time have learnt to play the harp very well, though she has only had some months' tuition, but she has great taste. All things to the greater glory of God. Remember we sail D.V. from Liverpool on the 14th of this month. I hope there will not be any disarrangement by our going back, no more than if we were returning from Guelph or Hamilton, although it may be the feast of St. Teresa. The Nuns from the missions will have plenty to do by that time. Give them all my love.

Yours fondly in J. C.,

M. J. TERESA.

140

LORETTO CONVENT, BOND STREET

So the summer was over and when the travellers reached home the rejoicing may be imagined by those whose friends have gone away for a time, far beyond the horizon, and who returned ere the sighing for their departure had quite died away. Indeed in those days, although swift steamers plied the briny deep, still the immediate assurance of the well being of the absent was not so easily obtainable as to-day, for there was neither cable nor wireless in operation, and so anxiety and suspense had to be satisfied with news two weeks old. What must have been the joy then in the dear old Convent on again seeing the returned Foundress at home.

Of this Loretto of St. Ignatius there are the fondest recollections, for was it not the first house the beloved early members could call their own, was it not planned and built by the saintly Rev. Mother Teresa, who spent so many years of her life in happy toil and labour within its sacred precincts, teaching her children the nothingness of this world and the glory of the reward which she and so many loved Religious trained by her have attained. All the previous abodes of the Community were rented houses, so this was the first real home, and it might be called the cradle of the Institute; for how many look back to the day and the hour when in the devotional little Chapel in the Presence of the All-Holy, they made their formal act of renouncement of all that the world holds dear. The story is told of a Novice in the middle '70's who, after having long sought the permission of her parents to embrace the Religious life, and it seemed that there was not even the possibility of a hope of ever obtaining it, entered

141

at the age of twenty-four, with the highest expectations of realizing the ideals she had cherished so long. Three nights after she had put on the Postulant's garb the door bell of the Convent on Bond St. rang very loudly, and a gentleman stood at the entrance, who in not very low tones announced that he had come to take his daughter home. He was shown into the little parlour, and when Rev. Mother Teresa received his message from the Portress she calmly said, "Send Sister N. to him." The poor Postulant on her part was greatly frightened and begged Rev. Mother to send some Sisters to the chapel to say the Rosary for her. Her request was granted and she was advised to remove her Postulant cap lest the sight of it should exasperate her angry father, and to await God's pleasure. The meeting was stormy and pathetic, between the father, who felt that his wishes were not consulted, and the daughter who, although possessed of the tenderest filial affection, felt that she was following the Will of God. When the former had exhausted all arguments, and his throat seemed parched, the daughter offered to fetch him a glass of water, and coming out into the hall managed to secure a little bottle of Lourdes' water from which she poured a drop or two into the glass she had just filled, with which she returned to the parlour.

With trembling hand the poor father seized the glass, and looking into the face of his child which was wet with tears, he swallowed the contents. Scarcely had he done so when a calmness passed over his face, and although he did not speak for some moments, his anger had died away, and the daughter felt that a miraculous change had taken place, and that Our Lady had gained a member for her Institute. The victory was won, but the parting was not yet. However, when it did come, instead of trying to force her home, he gave her his blessing, with full permission to remain in Loretto. The father departed, his heart wrung with grief, but it was a grief that lessened daily until his sacrifice became to him a matter of joy. And how fared it with his child? Day by day she seemed to grow holier, and in her, filial affection was so strong that it was surpassed only by the love of God. Happy was it for her that it was thus, for her years in Religion were few, and a bright crown had to be won in a short space of time. A year or two after her holy Profession, after only a few days' illness she succumbed to an attack of pneumonia, having edified all by the holiness of her life. Indeed the perfume of her virtues still remains. How consoling to the Chief Superior amid her manifold duties were such choice vocations, and still, when even the most desirable sought admission, she showed no unseemly haste and left all to the guiding finger of God.

The Convent on Bond St. was much enlarged in later years, very solid additions had to be made to accommodate the large classes in attendance, and although another domicile was provided for the boarders before five years of its existence had passed, still it continued to be the residence of Rev. Mother Teresa and Community, including the Novitiate, for many years. This fact has given it a larger place in the affections of the members of the Institute than many of the more imposing edifices more recently established. For many of the Religious look back and speak of what is now known as the Nazareth of the Institute as a veritable Paradise in the earlier days, where so many remembrances of the saintly Foundress abound in Chapel, and hall and oratory. But no man can stay the hand of Time and the world moves on; what was once a desirable residential portion of the city has deteriorated greatly and the school has practically finished its course. But the memories of the religious life of that house will ever be enshrined in the grateful hearts of the Sisters, who there first tasted the sweetness of the spiritual atmosphere perfumed with so many virtues. Looking back at the prosperous years of '65 and '66, it is seen that the burning desire of the Religious seemed to be to procure more ample accommodation for the souls committed to their charge in Toronto, but a most favourable opening in another city presented itself before the tastes and requirements of the Toronto Community could be satisfied in the Queen city.

CHAPTER XIV

LORETTO CONVENT, HAMILTON. PATRONS. VOCATIONS. SUCCESS OF SCHOOLS.

IN 1865 Rt. Rev. Bishop Farrell of Hamilton wrote to Rev. Mother Teresa suggesting to her a beautiful place in sight of the mountain, and overlooking Burlington Bay for a future Loretto Convent. His Lordship expressed regret, that he was not then able to purchase the property to offer it as a gift, but fully realizing the benefits the childrn of his diocese in Guelph were reaping from the labours of the Nuns, he made an effort not to let the desirable place fall into other hands. A fairly commodious house stood at the head of a green-wooded lawn, that was surrounded by a box hedge, shutting off a fine orchard on one side, and a garden that was a veritable bower of roses on the other. This valuable site was purchased by the Community for the modest sum of eight thousand dollars, but of course, as in many other cases, large sums had to be expended on what was merely a cosy residence, to render it fit for the reception of boarders, and a Chapel had to be at once erected for the Master. The Religious found sleeping accommodation over what once was a stable, and some testify that it seemed as if the sun rose there over the ambitious city, for rays of light came direct through the roof at dawn, hence the name Rue Celeste. Under the Chapel were built the large spacious class rooms of to-day, and on the eve of the Exaltation of the Holy Cross, the mission of Mount St. Mary, under the patronage of Mater Admirabilis, was established. Rt. Rev. Dr. Farrell had been most anxious that all due precaution should be taken for the permanence and stability of the foundation, as the following letter will show:

HAMILTON, 2nd June, 1865.

Rev. Mother Superior,—

In answer to your letter of yesterday, I have no hesitation in consenting to have your houses in this diocese dependent on the Mother House of Toronto, so that the Superior of the latter house may be enabled to remove or change subjects, whenever she may deem it advisable, and that she may receive from the revenues of each establishment all due support for the said Mother house.

It is, moreover, my intention, that the house to be established in Hamilton shall be exempted from attending parochial offices, and shall be provided with daily Mass, weekly Confession, and the other opportunities of spiritual advancement usual in your Communities, and in conformity with the spirit of the Church.

Faithfully yours in X. T.,

+ JOHN B.P., OF HAMILTON.

We have seen how this letter wisely arranged the union of the Hamilton foundation with the Mother House in Toronto, or rather agreed to it, for Rev. Mother Teresa took care for the future, as well as for the present, that if possible no stumbling block should interfere with its progress; and that a proper under-

146

standing from the first with the Chief Pastor, was the surest way to ensure success. The good Prelate, with a large heart, saw that everything was done for the temporal and spiritual welfare of the Nuns inasmuch as lay in his power, and indeed the provision of a Chaplain was a boon which lasted not only during his life but continued after his death. Rev. Mother Teresa went to Hamilton for the opening to see that all was as comfortable and convenient for the Nuns as possible, and with her were Mother M. Stanislaus Hennigan, Sister M. Aloysius, and two others. All these were considered good teachers, as well as good Religious, and so, leaving Mother Stanislaus in charge, the Chief Superior returned to Toronto, feeling that she had accomplished the task of founding what promised to be a very fruitful mission. Nor indeed was she in any sense disappointed. As in other parts of Ontario the Protestants were, of course, the wealthier class; the most socially prominent among them were pleased to place their daughters in charge of the Nuns, and proved sincere, loyal friends of the Institution from the very first. It is quite certain that at one time Protestants were numerically greater at the Academy than Catholics, but as the years went on, the numbers of the latter increased, and choice vocations came from the best families of the ambitious city. There was one unique feature, however, about this establishment, and it was this—not only the élite of Protestant society patronized the Academy, but the daughters of Protestant clergymen were among the cherished pupils of the Convent. One Protestant lady whose three daughters were educated there never

failed to send her floral offering to the Chapel at
Christmas and Easter; and at entertainments and receptions at which she was an honoured guest, it was
good to see her stately form and animated features
with a smile of approbation for what was rare, or
true, or beautiful. Through her influence, direct or
indirect, many besides her own children found their
way to the Convent, and are now pursuing honourable
careers in the world. She was most careful in the
education of her children, and daily for years her
private carriage conveyed her cherished daughters,
from their stately home on the mountain to the Convent, where they were to remain until the coachman
came at five to take them home. Then after leaving
school and having been presented at Court, and having
entered on their social career, matters concerning their
success were communicated to the Nuns with most
kindly sincerity, as to persons who were not insensible
to the joys and sorrows of those who had once been
their pupils. This lady never embraced the true faith,
although she seemed to stand ever within its shadow.
The Catholics of Hamilton have always taken a reasonable pride in the success of this Institution and the
clergy from the first have been most faithful in their
spiritual ministrations. Miracles of grace have been
wrought within its walls and conversions of entire
families have followed the entrance of pupils in this
Academy in the not very remote past. The hearing
of some of these cases was a very great consolation to
Rev. Mother Teresa, as her zeal for souls increased
with the years of her life, but her principle ever was
that real success was only achieved through humility,

and while it naturally afforded her much pleasure to know that the Nuns were successful in their work and were appreciated by those for whom they laboured, yet what seemed to delight her most was that they merited it.

Hamilton Academy has long since celebrated its silver jubilee and its record has kept improving in every respect. The old house stands yet at the head of the lawn, but a new structure, built at its side, to meet all modern requirements, is much in evidence from the driveway that leads to the entrance. From Chicago and other American cities have come the children of Canadian mothers who were educated at this Loretto, and who think that no Loretto can compare with their Alma Mater. Rt. Rev. Dr. Dowling, the incumbent of the Episcopal See for nearly a quarter of a century, has ever been a true friend to the Institute, and for the Nuns who have worked for the children of his Episcopal See, he has always the highest encomiums. One incident of his fatherly care in the recent past might be here recorded which shows the shepherd's care for the sheep. One of the Hamilton Nuns who, although only of middle age, had been dying of heart trouble and feeling that if she visited the Falls Convent and breathed the air around the famous mound overhanging the Cataract, she would surely recover. obtained permission to carry out her desire. After her arrival, for a few days she seemed to convalesce, but the ebb soon followed the flow of life, and feeling that she was dying, although she had been previously anointed, a priest was hastily summoned to her bedside from Clifton. It happened that the Bishop of

Hamilton had administered the Sacrament of Confirmation on that day in St. Patrick's Church, Clifton, as the Pastor thought it too long for the children to delay the reception of the Sacrament until the appointment of His Grace Most Rev. N. McNeil, D.D., Archbishop of Toronto. Seated at dinner, surrounded by the clergy, the Bishop had communicated to him that a priest had to leave the table immediately to attend a Sister who was dying up at Falls View. On inquiry he found it was the Sister who had come from Hamilton only a short time before, and he at once announced that he also would go to see her. On arriving at the Convent he asked to be shown to the Nun's cell, and after having reached there, he knelt at the bedside of the dying Religious and gave her his last benediction. He then remarked she was a good Religious and that he knew her well, but alas, the tired eyes were closing and there was no sign of recognition from one who was ever grateful and appreciative of every spiritual favour. She had given herself to God in the very morning of life and reaped an early reward. She was named after the Chief Superior, Teresa in baptism, and had chosen for her name in Religion, St. Michael. It is fondly trusted that her namesake and the defender of the Institute rejoiced at her entrance into the Eternal Kingdom.

As in the case of other foundations a large separate school is attached to this Convent and Academy, and very satisfactory are the results of the departmental examinations. When this school was first offered to the Nuns, Rev. Mother Teresa was most solicitous as to the teachers she should send there, and indeed her interest never flagged, and sometimes when on visitation she presided at an examination in the Separate school, the teacher was at her wits' end to see that the children did not miss a single question asked them, for the limit of studies was considered very reasonable, and as the subjects studied were not numerous, the Chief Superior was of the opinion that these should be thoroughly known and assimilated.

But the virtues of the children were what always claimed her willing ear, and when any Mistress had something to relate which tended to show the docility, or obedience or charity of any pupil, then indeed her face beamed, and to help such a child in some practical way without particularly noticing her at the time was immediately her decision. How many such had reason to remember her visit we cannot say, for her left hand hardly ever seemed aware of the actions of the good right hand.

CHAPTER XV

LYNDIIURST LORETTO ABBEY. DIFFICUL-
TIES. FIRST MASS SAID IN FORMER
BALL ROOM. VISIT OF GOVENOR-
GENERAL AND HIS ROYAL CONSORT
PRINCESS LOUISE. LETTER ANNOUNC-
ING THE VISIT OF THE ABLEGATE DR.
CONROY.

REV. MOTHER TERESA returned to Toronto,
after having fairly launched the new Loretto
Hamilton, when it was more evident than ever that
another house in the Queen City was an urgent necessity, and so she deemed no time was to be lost if they
were to hold the children who had come to them ex-
pecting to find perfect accommodation. She had
always recourse to prayer as a first means to an end,
and as has been seen, with evident success. In one
of her exhortations to the Religious she said, "O, if
we only knew the gift of God, that the only way to
obtain it is through constant meditation on the attributes of God and prayer. 'Ask and you shall receive.' O how negligent we are in all that concerns our
most vital interest. Spouses of Jesus Christ, our one
desire should be the knowledge, love and service of
God." How ardently she then prayed for the means
to extend His kingdom in the hearts of those confided to her, but ever diffident and timid in character,
she consulted the Bishop as to what he thought the
best plan to pursue. He advised the purchase, if

possible, of some place with a building already on it, and large enough grounds on which to build in the future if further accommodation should be required. He impressed on her that there was no time to be lost, but he could not then think of any place available.

As a true child of obedience and full of zeal, immediately after the interview, she set out with Mother Joseph McNamara hoping that Providence would direct her steps to some such property as she desired, and prayed for. Indeed the purchase of the Abbey did in the end seem providential, although nothing came from this long search. In 1867 Rev. John Walsh, riding in the cars from St. Mary's, met a Catholic gentleman, Mr. Mulvey, who remarked to him, "Mrs. Widder's place is for sale, Mr. Merrick has told me. I think it would suit the Loretto Nuns perfectly," and turning to Mr. McDonald, a lawyer, he said, "This gentleman has the selling of it." Father Walsh, afterwards Bishop of London, and Archbishop of Toronto, one of the best friends of Loretto Nuns in all circumstances who had been Confessor and Chaplain to the Community for many years, lost no time in communicating to Rev. Mother Teresa the remark made by Mr. Mulvey, but as there was a mortgage on the place, a little fear was entertained about purchasing it. Daily were the Nuns watching and praying for a suitable site, and many other projects were formed for obtaining the desired abode but with little or no satisfaction. At length a letter came from Mr. Mulvey, who was a good practical business man, saying that Mrs. Widder's property was really purchasable, but unfortunately, Rev. Mother Teresa was in Hamilton when his letter came to Toronto, and she did not return until the day on which the sale was to take place. Great was her disappointment indeed when she found Mr. Mulvey's letter awaiting her at Bond St. Convent, as she realized that the most eligible site in Toronto had probably passed beyond her reach. Nevertheless, urged by her great need, she determined to call on Mr. Mulvey to find out if the sale had actually taken place on the appointed day according to the advertisement. Mr. Mulvey, who had the experience of the ways of the world, assured her that it had, as it was a chancery sale, and had to take place as advertised. However, he said since she seemed so anxious he would go down and enquire, so as to be absolutely certain. On his return he informed her, that contrary to his expectations, the sale was postponed till the following Saturday. This good news was communicated to Father Walsh and Rev. F. Jamot, a true friend and father to the Community. But another difficulty arose, the Bishop was absent, they knew not whether in Quebec or Montreal, and so immediate communication could not be had with him. In their perplexity recourse was had to prayer, Rev. Father Jamot, Rev. M. Teresa, M. M. Ignatia, M. M. Joseph, and M. M. Gonzaga knelt down in the parlour where the conversation was held. Then Father Jamot asked the Religious assembled if they would venture to incur a debt of sixteen thousand dollars, in the absence of the Bishop. All unhesitatingly said "Yes," knowing that His Lordship would be perfectly satisfied and very much pleased. The Vicar General, the kind friend of the Community, added that if the place could not be purchased for sixteen thousand dollars he would venture to bid eighteen thousand, trusting that the Bishop would not think him too rash. While the matter was pending, many prayers were offered, especially on Saturday, the 6th February, 1867. Father Jamot said Mass that morning at the Convent for the success of the affair. When the time for the sale arrived, all parties needed were easily found, and the property was sold at the first bid made by Mr. Mulvey for the Nuns. This seemed providential to Rev. Mother Teresa, and so she lost no time in securing what God seemed to intend specially for her Community. But still there was difficulty in obtaining possession. Lyndhurst, as the place was called, was then one of the most desirable residences in Toronto, and with extreme regret, if not actual repugnance, the Mistress consented to its transfer to a Religious Community. Indeed she seemed very reluctant to leave the abode, where she seems to have lived in semi-regal state, considering herself above the élite of Toronto, inviting principally, it was said, the military to the balls and social functions at what was then considered her palatial residence. Her daughter informed the Nuns that her brother who was then in England had a lease of the place for two years, and that it had not yet expired, moreover he had charged his lawyer not to let the property go at any price. Providence, however, seemed to have overruled these plans. Finally, they refused to give possession of the house unless carpets and other furnishings were bought, and to this Rev. Mother Teresa agreed in order to move more quickly into the place so badly needed by the Community. Rev. Mother's first care was to prepare a place for the reception of the Blessed Sacrament, and the most beautiful room of the house, the ball room, with it Corinthian pillars, and handsome decorations, was selected. Here Bishop Lynch said Mass on the 8th September, 1867, and Lyndhurst was of the past, and Loretto Abbey of the Holy Family was established. On the 22nd of the same month, the Bishop solemnly blessed the house, and many of the citizens attended the ceremony, walked in the procession, and assisted at the Benediction of the Blessed Sacrament given on the spacious verandah at the head of the steps leading to the grounds. The Bishop wished a beautiful stained glass window with the Widder Arms and the motto, "Nusquam meta mihi"* to be left in its place over-looking the hall, as a portion of the "spoils of Egypt" and a trophy of the victory gained by Religion over the world. In this lofty spacious hall the band, which was always in attendance at Mrs. Widder's balls, had been accustomed to be stationed, and there was set up the statue of St. Michael, the defender. The scene was changed. There was no longer the sound of revelry by night, and to use Gerald Griffin's words, "the feast was forsaken for fasting and prayer" though not by the revelers. The other parts of the house were by no means suited to the requirements of a boarding school, as all the boarders had to be removed from Bond St. to make room for the pupils of the crowded day school, and as the former young ladies found them-

---

*Literally nowhere limit to me.

LORETTO ABBEY, TORONTO.

selves in very close quarters, in this fashionable residence, they did not so greatly appreciate the change. Hence we find in less than four years that on Sept. 14th, 1871, Archbishop Lynch was again performing another ceremony at the Abbey in laying the corner stone of the new Chapel dedicated to the Holy Family under the patronage of St. Teresa. His Grace officiated on this occasion, with all the dignity and piety which characterized him as a Prelate, and he was assisted by the Very Rev. Y. Jamot, Very Rev. Father Rooney, V.G., Very Rev. Dean Proulx, and a number of the clergy of the diocese. Then followed a procession of the Nuns and pupils, after which Ven. Archdeacon Northgraves delivered a most impressive sermon, and the proceedings terminated by Benediction of the Most Blessed Sacrament. A beautiful recreation and examination hall had been built at the same time as this Chapel, but three other structures have been added since; and although the present Abbey now forms but an insignificant part of the original building that crowned the once exclusive Lyndhurst on Wellington Place, still in the eyes of those who lived and struggled with Rev. Mother Teresa in the early days, pleasant memories linger around the much coveted prize, for which the Foundress had worked and prayed. In February, 1877, she moved the Novitiate from Bond St. to the Abbey which has since been the Mother House of the Institute in America.

In the '70's and '80's of the last century Rev. Mother Teresa took an active part in the education of the children of the schools at the Abbey, as well as in those of the Novitiate, and, in imparting religious instruction, she was particularly happy, for there are those yet living who remember well the disappointment of the young ladies when the beloved instructress, called away on some urgent business, would depute someone to take her place, although this feeling, on the part of the children, was never allowed to find expression in words. The importance of this work of religious instruction was ever impressed on the Nuns, by Rev. Mother Teresa, and she always seemed animated and in a measure, inspired, when speaking of the need of catechetical instruction. Indeed a letter written to one of the Religious at this time shows how fully she esteemed the privilege of having received instructions from a holy Jesuit Father on the subject:

LORETTO ABBEY, TORONTO.
(Undated.)

My Dear Sister M.,—

Trusting to your great zeal for the honour of St. Francis Xavier, I want you to heighten his accidental glory by offering a holy violence to Heaven during the ten Fridays in order to obtain through his intercession, the grant of an important request connected closely with the interests—the best interests of our holy Institute. Will you ask all our dear Sisters at the Falls to pray that our children may be good, and that we may all, at all times, keep in view the main object—our own salvation, and that of those priceless souls confided to our trust—holy but momentous charge? Thanks to the splendid instruction of holy Father Holzer on the subject of catechism, I feel the weight of this duty. He exhorted us to look to the religious instruction of the children above all things, and said that all other useful science would be promoted by that, as when the children are pious they will be industrious and obedient. Let us for ourselves and children seek first the kingdom of God and His glory, and all these things shall be added unto us, for He Who is disposed to give us what is greatest will not refuse us that which is least, if it be beneficial to us. I have not heard from Ireland since. I send this by our dear kind Father. Pray for me.

Yours fondly in J. C.,

M. J. TERESA.

This was the main object of the existence of the Institute and hence of this she never lost sight. But everything that contributed to the education and refinement of the pupils appealed strongly to her aesthetic sense. Any praise of the pupils coming from authority she respected, touched a deep responsive chord in her heart, and hence we find her writing to a friend overseas, on the occasion of His Excellency, Dr. Conroy, visiting the Abbey.

LORETTO ABBEY, WELLINGTON PLACE,
TORONTO, 17th August '77.

My Own Dear M.A.,—

It is long since I wrote to you, too long, and the same may be said of my hearing from you. Dear M.M.A. wrote to me since you did, so that I heard from Rathfarnham, but even this is a long time since. I feel that I may blame myself or rather my silence. We have had a great deal to do for some months past,

159

and the vacation is nearly over, it has passed for me in constant occupation.

On Tuesday, the 24th June, we had a most delightful visit from His Excellency, Dr. Conroy, Papal Ablegate, accompanied by His Grace, the Archbishop. They called at the Abbey about noon. Considerable preparation had been made, as was most meet, for the reception of the representative of our beloved Holy Father. The grounds were in beautiful order and looked their very best for the occasion. The Chapel, halls and reception rooms had been tastefully decorated with mottoes, flowers, wreaths, etc. On entering the Abbey His Excellency first proceeded to the Chapel where the Te Deum was sung. He then received the Nuns, when each one was presented to him in turn, and for each he had a kind word and a gracious smile. The pupils, dressed in white, were waiting for His Excellency in the large reception hall. When he entered the children played a march on two pianos and two harps. The programme comprised the "O Gloriosa Domina," "God Bless Our Pope," "The Exile of Erin," and "Irish Airs." A poem on the Pope's Jubilee was recited by three little girls, and was very much admired. A few appropriate words were spoken in presenting a bouquet of flowers. In the address, read by one of the larger girls, a touching allusion was made to His Excellency's being no stranger in Loretto. I wish I could produce verbatim his beautiful reply. He complimented the children very highly and encouraged them to the acquisition of every virtue becoming a Christian young lady. He quoted the address, saying he was no stranger in Loretto, and said he was delighted to find the same spirit here that he admired elsewhere—the spirit and the action of educating the young—a work especially dear to the heart of the Holy Father—that he was reminded of the earthly Trinity, the family of Nazareth, that he found the sweet face of Mary in the modesty of the Nuns, the tender smile of Jesus in the countenances of the children, and the protecting care of Joseph ever in the house of Nazareth, that house that had been translated from Palestine to Europe by the hands of Angels—but here he found himself in presence of a more striking miracle, here, too, the angels had been at work transferring the home of earthly gaiety into a Sanctuary of God (alluding to the special Providence that guided us in the purchase of the Abbey). The children were all presented formally and were charmed with the kindness and courtesy of the Delegate.

He took special notice of the little children who were delighted with his fatherly manner towards them. He went from group to group seeming really anxious to grant them some favour. The vacation was so near that a holiday would be quite commonplace, so he granted a Silver Medal for Christian Doctrine, and this was regarded as the highest prize on the list. The Delegate remarked that the children were extremely ladylike, and he repeated this more than once.

*   *   *   *   *   *

In September, '79, the Abbey was in a thrill of expectation over the reception of Her Royal Highness, the Princess Louise, and her noble Consort, the

Marquis of Lorne, the then Governor-General of Canada. Rev. Mother Teresa was deeply interested in all the preparations made to receive their Excellencies. As their visit to Toronto had been postponed from May until September, and the day on which it was appointed they should honour Loretto Abbey by their presence, was the tenth, when the pupils would have only entered on the new term, her anxiety that the reception and school entertainment given to the distinguished guests would be in some measure worthy of them, was quite evident. On the eventful day, the Welcome Song, Address and Music bespoke the hearty loyalty and reverence for authority which she ever inculcated, and the smile of approval the gracious Princess was indeed a welcome tribute to the humble hostess. The affability of Her Royal Highness, the Princess Louise, and her apparent interest in the appointments of the house, gave Rev. Mother Teresa much pleasure, and she often admiringly commented on the wisdom of the Governor-General's speech in answer to the addresses of the pupils. Every word in appreciation of Convent education was music to her ears, and all the sweeter when it was uttered with evident sincerity on the part of the speaker, particularly when he spoke of the loftiness of the motive of the teachers.

After the entertainment in the reception room was over, the Chapel, dormitories, Nuns' Corridors and Studio were visited by Their Excellencies, accompanied by Rev. Mother and a word of praise for the beauty of the little Chapel, which appealed to Her Royal Highness, fell on a very appreciative ear. The view of the grounds from the upper windows was greatly admired, and the blue lake stretching away to the horizon enhanced the beauty of the scene. Sometime after this visit a letter from the Governor-General's Secretary announced that Loretto Abbey was to be the recipient of a medal presented by His Excellency, the Governor-General, to the pupil most proficient in any study selected by the Nuns. English Literature was chosen, and the presentation of the prize competed for is annually a grateful reminder of Their Excellencies' visit.

Sometime in April the following year the young lady pupils of the Abbey were invited to spend a few hours at Government House by the Misses McDonald, daughters of the Lieutenant-Governor, who, from their coming to Toronto, had evinced much friendship for the Community. The students were exceedingly pleased with the graciousness of their reception by the first ladies of Ontario, and a few days before the departure of the Lieutenant-Governor, who was replaced by Hon. Beverley Robinson, a farewell entertainment was given by the Abbey children to the ladies of the family of the outgoing Lieutenant-Governor, as a mark of the esteem they were held in by the Religious. In this same year the Society of the Living Rosary was established among the children by Rev. Father Gavan, the Chaplain, who did all in his power to promote the spiritual advancement of the pupils, and long are the accounts of the practices of devotions and processions in honour of the Heavenly Queen the May following. Rev. Mother's unceasing care for the welfare of the bodies and souls of the children was most marked, and great was her delight at the honour shown to the Heavenly Queen by Mary's children, but she was not unobservant of their little faults. A child who was troublesome, was invariably taken to accompany her in making the way of the Cross bearing her candle or assisting her in some way, or at times she would have her read from a spiritual book to her; and those so favoured were invariably so impressed with her patience and piety as to cease offending, and the fruit of her instruction was soon visible. She was clear sighted in almost all things but in the matter of vocation, she seemed to be inspired. Two young pupils who were greatly indulged by their father came habitually late after summer vacation, an irregularity which Rev. Mother could not condone, but which she excused with the hope of amendment. One of the Nuns tried to palliate this breach of discipline by remarking to Rev. Mother how the younger child on her return seemed almost as glad as a Religious would be to get back to the Convent after her long holiday spent at the seaside, when Rev. Mother interposed, "But nevertheless it is L— will become a Religious. M— has no vocation." The Religious had not long to wait to see the prediction verified, for the elder girl entered the next year, and has happily served God in Religion many years, while the younger soon became settled in the world.

In May, '81, the first Canadian Postulant, Sister Joseph McNamara, a model of obedience, and of many another virtue, after a well spent life, went to her reward, having passed thirty-two years in the Institute with edification to all. Rev. Mother might well have envied this first spiritual daughter of hers who had thus happily closed her career and gained her crown, while she had to meet new exigencies and float the banner of education over distant fields ere she could claim the reward of the "well done of the Master." In June 6th of the same year came a decree of His Holiness appointing Rev. Mother Teresa Chief Superior of the Institute in America. Her successors, lawfully elected, to bear the same title. His Grace Archbishop Lynch visited the Abbey on that occasion, and offered Mass in thanksgiving for the Papal Decree which he announced in the Chapel after the Gospel; afterwards he visited the schools and granted a holiday in honour of the favour of His Holiness. Meanwhile the want of accommodation for Nuns and pupils was again forcing itself on the Foundress, and a new wing to be built on the east side was occupying her thoughts as the easiest solution of the problem.

The feast of the Patron saint of the Foundress, the 15th of October, was celebrated with great éclat this year of '81. As the singing was conducted by Professor Torrington, who was the vocal instructor at the Abbey at the time, the Religious endeavoured to have a more varied programme than they might otherwise have had owing to the fact that the Mistress of Music's time was so fully occupied with the supervision of the instrumental selections on piano and harp that she could not pay much attention to the vocal. On this annual Feast it was customary for all the local Superiors to come to the Abbey from the mission houses, and bring with them whatever was rarest in needlework or art done by the Nuns, and this exhibition was a unique feature of the celebration, not less deserving of praise than the school entertainment. For all these marks of devotedness, the Foundress was always grateful, and happy were the remembrances carried away of her appreciation of the efforts that were put forth to honour her Patron saint. The religious part was what appealed most strongly to her, the singing of the children in the Chapel in congregational style, even before the "motu proprio" of His Holiness Pope Pius X. But joy or sadness had no visible effect on her self-control which was perhaps the virtue the Foundress possessed in the highest degree, in reality a combination of the virtues of humility, patience and meekness, it would seem. On the occasion of a small fire breaking out in the sanctuary, she remained calmly in her place at prayer before the Altar, and saw, with no signs of alarm on her face, the others rush to extinguish it, which, as she afterwards remarked, she knew they would do more easily and readily by her remaining at her place, and not hindering the activities of those busily engaged.

A pupil who had once made some disparaging remarks by way of comparison between the accommodation and convenience of one of the Loretto Convents, and a Convent she had previously attended, evidently annoyed a Sister who reported the matter to Rev. Mother Teresa. When she had finished, the Foundress very sweetly smiled and said, "Perhaps she said that to tease you!" And it really looks as if she had succeeded, from your disturbed demeanour. "But then," she remarked quietly, "the young lady is here because her parents were not satisfied with her progress in a certain branch of her studies. I hope the Nuns will give particular attention to that, and not blame the child for preferring a place to which she had been accustomed from her earliest school days." The young lady afterwards entered the Institute in Toronto, and was almost inconsolable when obliged to leave through ill health. And so it was always with Rev. Mother Teresa. There was no sign of disturbance or excitement, whatever occurred, but invariably after some untoward circumstance had come under her notice, she would investigate with a view to finding out the exact condition of affairs and then would seek a remedy, with the wisdom and calmness for which she was noted. When regret was sometimes expressed for the loss of a pupil from the school or a Postulant from the Novitiate, her usual remark was, "The Lord gave and the Lord has taken away, and the Lord will provide." Nor was her faith disappointed. "The Blessed are never disappointed, because they do not expect," and Reverend Mother neither wished nor expected anything but what God willed, and this was sure to come to pass.

Meanwhile Rev. Mother Teresa's time between the instructions given to Nuns and pupils of the Mother House, the Reception and Profession of members, and the visitations of the distant and near Convents of the Order, was fully occupied, but the want of accommodation at the Abbey forced itself on her and the crowded condition of the dormitories, class rooms and refectories, had to receive immediate attention. Even the beautiful little Chapel, which had elicited praise from a Princess for its tasteful decorations and architectural excellence, was found to be too small for the increased number of worshippers, and if there was any part of the house, in which Rev. Mother Teresa was more than ordinarily solicitous for good light and air, and plenty of room for the pupils, it was that sanctuary of peace blessed with the presence of the Most Holy.

CHAPTER XVI

THE NEW CHAPEL. AN EXAMPLE OF THE OBEDIENCE OF THE FOUNDRESS.

AGAIN in 1882 another new temple was raised to God, and while tradition is held sacred in Loretto, this building will be a monument to one of the most striking virtues of the Foundress. The old residence of Mrs. Widder, which formed the nucleus of the group of buildings that now constitute the Abbey, was of white brick or light in colour, and to harmonize with this and to give expression to the purity of the temple that was in her mind, Rev. Mother had a new Chapel commenced with the same material. Her one thought in those days was of the beauty and fairness of this structure which she had long since contemplated, and which had already reached the first story, when Archbishop Lynch called, and expressed his utter dissatisfaction with the plan and colour of the edifice. The former she could not altogether change, although that too was modified, but red brick replaced the white in the second and higher stories, and onlookers wondered at the contrast and sometimes enquired why two colours were used in the same building. When the edifice was completed, the ground walls were painted red to suit the colour of the upper part, and as time went on, and the once exclusive Lyndhurst property received a great deal of the dust and grime of traffic, the wisdom of the Prelate's suggestion was manifest, and no one more freely admitted the benefit of the change than Rev. Mother Teresa.

But the modification of the plan never entirely pleased her, and what was to be the culmination of her hopes that a not altogether unworthy temple should be raised by her to the Most High proved in reality a source of disappointment and deep concern to her. The humiliation was borne without a word, but when the Chapel was finished, and did not satisfy her aspirations she could not refrain from seeking the opinions of some cultured persons as to the impression made on them by the interior. The mother of one of the Religious who had seen many beautiful temples in Washington and New York consoled her not a little, by expressing, if not praise, at least a commendation of some of its unique features. The change of colour made no difference in the exterior for after having been painted it was never noticed, but the Chapel itself was not the one of her dreams, and the only comfort she derived from speaking of it was when someone found in it some architectural beauty or adornment which escaped her notice. She never ceased trying to decorate the sanctuary. She passed hours before the Blessed Sacrament and there she was to be found at any hour of the day when not actively engaged. Indeed, when at times it was difficult to find her, and one asked another if she knew where Rev. Mother might be, the usual answer was, "Have you been in the chapel?"

Had she lived to see the beautiful Chapel that commemorated the golden jubilee of the advent of the Nuns her joy would have been great, and her aesthetic sense satisfied, but alas! it was in this Chapel of her cherished hopes her body was laid for awhile before it was carried to its final resting-place.

CHAPTER XVII

FOUNDATION OF LINDSAY. "THE HIGHER
EDUCATION." REV. FATHER STAF-
FORD. LINDSAY CONVENT ON FIRE.

IN 1874 a very pressing invitation was extended to
Rev. Mother Teresa to send a little colony of her
then well-known Community to Lindsay, a rising,
prosperous town on the Scugog River, which derived
not a little of its fame from its pastor, the Canadian
Temperance Apostle, Rev. Father Stafford. Nor was
it in temperance alone that Father Stafford was deeply
interested; the question of education was to him a
very vital one, for the uplifting of his people was his
one absorbing thought. Indeed, among the professors
and teachers of Ontario of every creed and shade of
opinion he was justly looked up to, and his decisions
on matters educational were rarely questioned. Every
one knew the honesty of the man who was fearless
and outspoken in public as well as in private, while
his own people fairly idolized him. He was determined to have an educational institution of the very
first order in his own town, and so to bring the
"higher education" within the reach of the greater
number of his children. He had set his heart on getting the Loretto Nuns to take charge of this institution and with this end in view called on Archbishop
Lynch, who, he thought, might further his plans for
gaining the desired end. The Prelate told him he did
not think it probable that the Loretto Community

would send out any members to take charge of the really beautiful Convent which he had built, and advised him to seek another Community, which might possibly be glad of the opportunity offered. Nothing daunted, Father Stafford then asked him if he would approve of a branch of Loretto being established in his town in case he obtained the consent of Rev. Mother Teresa. The kindly Prelate said he would raise no objection to the Nuns undertaking this new enterprise if the members were numerous enough to warrant such a step. Indeed, he was better than his word, and greatly admiring the persistence of the priest in what he deemed was for the benefit of his people, he immediately called on Rev. Mother Teresa, and advised her if possible to send some members of her Community to Father Stafford, remarking at the same time, that whatever the zealous priest undertook generally prospered.

But there was some difficulty in persuading the Foundress to consent to what she deemed a departure from the beaten path in the region of education. The perfect polish in English and the accurate knowledge of French and other languages, as well as proficiency in music, for which her pupils were noted, would have to be sacrificed, she thought, for higher mathematics and shifting knowledge in science, and being naturally very conservative, she dreaded making any change in the educational programme of the Institute in America. Indeed, the students who then crowded the halls of her Academy in Toronto had no wish for a change, and certificates from the Department of Education or Matriculation passes were not desired by

172

them. First of all came the thought, would these innovations bring the children nearer to God? Well, the Archbishop expressed a desire to have the Lindsay mission established, and to her obedient soul, that wish was as a guiding star, knowing his deeply religious nature, his piety and learning she felt sure that she ran no risk in carrying it out. Then, too, she argued with herself, or rather against herself, that it might be well to have one house in Ontario where the pupils who so desired it could follow the course prescribed by the Department of Education and obtain their certificate of qualification Then, if a young lady desiring to be a teacher, applied to any of the other houses to enter as a pupil, with a view to following this course, she might be recommended to Lindsay. So she won a victory over herself, ever mindful of that petition of the "Our Father," "Thy Kingdom Come." The Archbishop was greatly pleased with this decision, and with the foresight for which he was ever remarkable, told the Community that this new departure might in a few years be a real necessity, for the idea of the "higher education" for girls was spreading, and so he counselled Rev. Mother Teresa to find at once suitable members for this foundation, and said he was ready to give his blessing to the work. It seems almost childish now, when one looks at the great fear that then existed about taking up this course, but there is no doubt of its having existence for there are those still living who remember what a shiver the thought that perhaps they might be chosen for Lindsay caused them. When it was whispered in the Novitiate that this new mission to carry on higher education was

soon to leave for Lindsay, the Ribadeneira of the
Novitiate instead of tripping persons on the stairs,
beckoned to a Postulant to take one end of her harp
while she took another, and having mounted the steep
stairs to the Cupola, commenced to accompany the
rhyme on "Lindsay and the Higher Education" which
she had composed, on the instrument. She had got
as far as the couplet:

"And now we come to Lindsay, of wide and high
     renown,
For all the wisdom of the world is centered in that
     town."

When the Novice Mistress hearing strains from the
upper regions, appeared on the scene, and looking
gravely at the harp, asked her how it happened to be
there. The witty rhymester told her that the feat had
been accomplished without a breach of silence, where-
upon the Mistress ordered her to carry the instrument
downstairs in the same manner, and that perhaps she
might give an exhibition of her musical and poetical
skill before Rev. Mother. When the matter was
explained to Rev. Mother Teresa as her sense of
humour was keen, she asked to hear the lines, and on
learning of the absurdities of the feats to be accomplished by higher education in Lindsay, laughed softly,
and told the Mistress to tell the Novice she would
prefer hearing a hymn accompanied on the harp.
Then the Foundress smilingly told the Community
that the cream would have to be skimmed for the new
mission, and nobody in this instance wished to be considered "la créme de la créme." Of course the Reli-

gious, at this time, were for the most part young ladies who had been educated in the different Convents of the Order, in the same manner precisely as their sisters who had entered society in the world, and to them who had never seen an inspector, or passed any other examination save that prescribed by the Nuns, the new state of affairs was something like an ordeal, but as Victor Hugo says, "Nous avons changé tout cela." Happily for the Community there were at the time a few who had, in addition to Convent training, Normal certificates and experience, and on them all eyes were speedily turned. For, at recreation was it not told that such a Sister not only had passed through the Normal school, but had distinguished herself there, as the records of that Institution still showed. Indeed, to that day her brilliant record might be read. Well, then, from different missions a little band had gathered at Loretto Abbey, there to await the final command to go forth. There was a great stir and brightness in the Abbey Community Room when all gathered for recreation, and some of the witty ones, who deemed themselves unqualified for the work, since they were not chosen, pleasantly addressed the outgoing with the spartan expression, "Go, my sister, return with your shield or upon it." In early September some finishing touches had yet to be put on the really elegant abode which good Father Stafford had prepared for the Nuns and their pupils, for as he deemed nothing intellectually too good for his people, so likewise he regarded nothing materially too good for the teachers of their children.

At the Mother House then the chosen few were

content to remain a little longer until everything was in readiness. But many thought Rev. Mother, in her own gentle way and with a gleam of that humour which seemed to be suppressed in her character, prepared them for the leaving in such a way that they did not sigh too much for the home left behind, and that in the end they were rather glad to meet the supposed danger. For whenever a supply was needed in the schools or a chaperon to accompany a child to the parlour, the Superior remembered them, and with a faint smile would say, "Perhaps Sister M. of the Lindsay Community might go." So from having been the "bete noire" of their existence, Lindsay became the mecca of their hopes, and gladly though timidly, they set forth at the voice of obedience to meet Father Stafford and the inspector. The distance from Toronto to Lindsay is not very great, and indeed even at that time had been spanned over by a railroad of moderate speed, but it was not the distance in space that the travellers had to pass over that impressed them, but the distance between schools that had been uninspected by seculars, and schools subject to such inspection. How graphically every item of interest that happened on the route was transmitted to Rev. Mother Teresa; and the magnificent reception accorded them by Father Stafford and his people lost nothing in the narration. The beautiful modernly equipped class rooms were fully described; and in those early times of rather primitive conveniences, marble basins and silver taps in dressing rooms for pupils were looked on somewhat as luxuries. Then came the children to fill the rooms, and of course the Nuns did not find them prodigies, but good, docile children who were willing and eager to learn not only what was duly prescribed for examinations, but whatever their instructresses thought best to impart, and truly those pupils must have been well impressed by their Pastor and parents as to the respect owing to religious teachers, for their reverence was very marked from the first. They were indeed a very fine type of Canadians, for as the Sister in charge of the schools remarked, "they were all of the class that sought the best," and Boston itself could not boast of a finer intellectual acumen than was developed on the banks of the Scugog. Father Stafford regularly visited the schools himself, and heard recitations in the different class rooms, but so searching were his questions, and so accurate the knowledge he required, that it might be safely surmised many prayers were offered for success when the teachers of the various rooms were anticipating his pastoral visit. On one occasion a Religious who taught French and music was congratulating herself on the fact that her children were doing very well, and that, as they were not following the regular course, they were exempt from giving an exhibition. Just as she had so expressed herself, M. M. Dosithea, the Superior, interposed, "Sister, the Priest is to hear your French class this morning at eleven." The Religious pleaded that she was nervous at the very thought, when the reverend clergyman came on the scene, and smilingly said, "Sister, we want brains here, not nerves." A look from the Head Mistress reassured her and she entered the class room, and after a most searching examination on the part of the examiner, in the conjugation of verbs, etc., it was ascertained that not a single mistake had been made by any pupil. The good Father, quite satisfied with results, when taking his departure asked a half holiday in the open air for teacher and pupils, "Just to brace their nerves."

Meanwhile Rev. Mother Teresa was very anxious lest the examination grind should in any way lessen the religious spirit of her daughters, and the following letter written to the Head Mistress about this time, shows exactly her sentiments:

LORETTO ABBEY,
TORONTO, 1st March, '77.

My Dearst Sister M.M.,—

I must begin by wishing you many graces during this season, doubly holy on account of Lent, and being the month of St. Joseph. The coming of these favoured times makes me sad lest we should not become better for them, because if we do not, we become worse, having more frustrate graces to answer for. This will not be your case, I fondly trust. Keep in sight the one thing worth your regard. I know you have many distracting cares, troublesome occupations; but out of these you have to work out your perfection and salvation; you see perfection goes before salvation.

We were glad to see Father Stafford. His sermon, or rather lecture, was very successful. Many were greatly pleased with it. The Archbishop is getting better. It may be long before he can venture to go about. We are all very grateful to God for His Grace's recovery, for we should have lost a kind father and friend in him. Tell M.M. that I would not want "to make her teeth water," as she would be likely to say herself; but we had a beautiful sermon from Father P. this morning on the means of doing penance without fasting or any other exterior mortification. I wish that I could give you a resumé of it, and induce you to put it in practice. Guard of the eyes and tongue was among the practices he recommended. He said we should look at Christ and then look at ourselves. We should by this see what was wanting to us, as Christ is the Model on which we must form ourselves. The sermon was in some respects an exposition of the seventeenth Rule. "Could you, my dear children," he said, "take up only one good habit during the Lent you would do much?" Unfortunately he did not remember that this was the first day of March or he would have given some advice as to the favours we should ask, and the most efficacious manner of obtaining them.

Poor M.P. is at the Falls still. She seems to get better very slowly. Get your children to pray for her and for M.E. Sr. M.E. and all are well, including myself.

Wishing you a holy Lent, and a happy Easter, I am, as ever,

Yours fondly in C. J.,

M. J. TERESA.

This letter, like many others of Rev. Mother Teresa, will show what the dominant note of her whole life was, aiming at her own perfection and salvation, and at the perfection and salvation of her spiritual

179

daughters. No matter what the work or the place, the ever abiding presence of God was to her the great reality, and while she busied herself with many other things, she always aimed at the one thing necessary. Only breaches of Rule or their results really troubled her. She rejoiced in the progress and success of the schools, but did not seem over anxious as to gratifying results. On one occasion she visited a Convent where one of the pupils expressed dissatisfaction as to her progress, and indirectly found fault with her teacher, who had taken the greatest possible trouble in advancing her interests. Rev. Mother was told she threatened to leave if her views were not considered. Taking out her watch, Rev. Mother said, "Is there a train this evening, and someone to accompany the young lady home? She should not be detained any longer than necessary." Next day after receiving some salutary advice, the pupil took her departure, and someone remarked it was better for all that she had gone since she was so ungrateful. Rev. Mother remarked, "Better for both," meaning the over zealous, kind teacher as well as the unappreciative pupil. The young lady lived to regret the step, and it may be said to her credit, she was perfectly frank afterwards in the acknowledgment of her mistake, and tried to show her gratitude both to the Religious and to the Institute in a thousand ways.

One of Rev. Mother Teresa's cardinal virtues was her absolute silence regarding the imperfections she or others might possibly have noticed in the members of the Community. Long after her death a Prelate remarked that when he was Parish Priest of ———, one of the Religious did something with regard to his school affairs which displeased him, although the matter did not involve even an imperfection on the part of the Sister, he felt bound to tell Rev. Mother that it was not according to his pleasure. She looked grieved and glancing at her companion said, "Oh," in a pained manner, but not a word escaped her. The one word expressed her sorrow for what had happened, but knowing that the Religious acted, as she thought justly, in the case, she would not condemn her. It was only one of the instances in which her charity was conspicuous, and this trait of reticence regarding the faults of others seemed in her to be both natural and supernatural. Her visits to Lindsay were joyous occasions to the Nuns and pupils as she was thoroughly appreciative of the work done by the Community along the lines of intellectual culture, and when she heard of some promising vocations among them, she felt that the religious training was not neglected, for her motto ever was, "A tree is known by its fruit." On her return to Toronto, how warmly and affectionately she spoke of these dear spiritual daughters who were working so nobly for God and the Institute in this new field, and how deeply grateful for the generosity they displayed in undertaking such difficult tasks for the greater glory of God. Indeed, this mission which she had looked on rather coldly at first, and had not undertaken only for the warm recommendation of Archbishop Lynch, proved one of the greatest blessings to the Institute of the future in Canada, for in it were first trained the zealous Religious who were capable of taking charge of what is called the "higher education" in the Academies and schools of the Institute in the province.

The first departmental test of the Lindsay school was, as is the case in most beginnings, rather disappointing in results, but it is an established fact that the young lady who obtained the highest grade certificate in that year became the first Postulant from Lindsay school, and has worked with marked success in the domain of higher education in fields not then dreamt of, and that she was the pioneer of hosts of others, the first and fairest of Lindsay's daughters. As the years went on, the number of the certificated increased, and this usually meant an increase in the Novitiate, until even Guelph vocations were outnumbered by those of Lindsay. Most of these are still in the zenith of their fame as teachers of the Institute, and it were invidious to select any names from among the groups of those who left all for God, in the very first spring of youth. Sometimes all the girls of a family embraced the religious life. But one now deceased some years who gave herself wholly to God in a marked manner in these early days deserves some passing notice.

Sr. M. Ethelreda Curtin was not only one of the first boarders in the Lindsay Convent, but was also a cherished child of Father Stafford's own flock. Hence her desire to enter the Institute met with his warmest approbation. He selected the name of the Saint she was to bear and blessed her in her choice of life. She had previously had Normal training and gained the highest marks in pedagogy. In the Novitiate her ability as a teacher was at once recognized and there her methods were generally assimilated. Though a born teacher, she was the most childlike and docile in that first school of religion, and no one seemed to make greater strides in that most difficult of sciences, the science of the Saints. Coming from the clear and invigourating air of Lindsay, one would naturally have expected to find her robust, but from the very first there was a frail look about her which some accounted for by her intense application to study. She had an ardent desire to persevere in her cherished vocation, and any allusion to an appearance of her delicacy of constitution called forth from her gentle remonstrances. To her religious life was particularly easy, and customs which proved a stumbling block to others, were adopted without apparently any trouble on her part. Thus joyous and free of care, she passed the morning of her life in religion, and any passing cloud was quickly dispersed by the sunshine of her nature. After the lapse of some years when no signs of regaining strength appeared, she was sent to Lindsay Convent for a change, hoping that her native air might work a charm. Then as she seemed a little stronger, she declared herself perfectly able and willing to work in the schools; to complete the cure, however, it was deemed advisable to place her on the Lindsay staff, but when she heard this announcement her grief was great, for she assured Rev. Mother that although she might possess many qualifications of a teacher, she could never satisfy the people of her native town, who had so admired and appreciated the first Nuns that they placed them on a plane far elevated above their immediate surroundings. The most distant field of

action which was then Joliet, she preferred to her home
town, where there might possibly be a chance of shat-
tering the ideals of her own townspeople. So sincere
was her representation that for the time at least she
was excused from being a prophet in her own country,
and a distant mission in which she did much for the
glory of God and the salvation of her neighbour,
claimed her most undivided attention. But not for
long. To the Mother House where she was fondly
remembered from her Novitiate days she soon returned, physically very weak but still determined to
persevere in her unceasing work. She became Mistress
in name of the middle school, and the children could
never think of her in any light but in that of a Saint.
Everything that could be done to lighten her duties
by the children of that unthinking age, was gladly
done by them, and indeed their souls in return must
have been benefited by the example of patience and
resigned cheerfulness which was ever present to them.
The charge was given her with the admonition
that she was never to preside for a long time but was
merely to act as supervisor, so that her influence in
the schools might not be wholly lost.

A dear friend, a Religious in one of the city houses,
about a week before her death, came to visit her, and
found her seated on a lounge in the Infirmary, very
little changed in appearance, and so did not dream that
she knew her end was so near. The visitor asked
incidentally if she had seen her parents lately, "Oh,
yes," she replied, "Father and mother came to the
city to stay for the end, and would you believe," she
added humourously, "that mother persuaded father to

go home as the waiting time might be too long for him, she thought. But this was really to give herself a longer time with me." She chatted pleasantly of past happy days in religion until her friend had to leave, then she inquired if her visitor expected to come again during the week, and having been assured that she possibly could not, she said, "Good bye until ———" and looking up, she indicated a meeting in Heaven. All this was in the calmest, most joyous manner. She was really the fairest fruit of Lindsay.

Meanwhile the work in the schools went on with gratifying results, and the good Pastor was unceasing in his endeavours to promote the cause of education. Some one remarked of him in looking at his well kept grounds that he never planted anything that did not grow and thrive, and this might have applied to the growth of an Institution as well as a tree or plant. He was delighted to bring his guests to see the establishment he had laboured to construct, and the good order of the children was to him a matter of no small pleasure. He had visited Europe once or twice, some thought in the interests of Temperance, others thought of Education, and indeed, in both these interests he worked, but a third and possibly chief interest to him, as was afterwards learnt, was that of his health, but his zeal for souls was not of any time or condition as the following incident will show: One morning he was taking some exercise on his grounds in pushing the lawn mower with great vigour, inside the fence which enclosed the Presbytery, when he noticed a man look across the barrier, who after having passed on to the end of the fence returned and saluted him in a friendly though unfamiliar style, "Good morning, Mr. Stafford." The manner of salutation showed the good Father that the speaker was not of the household of the faith, but he pleasantly answered the man, and enquired if he could do anything for him. After some hesitation, as if seeking an excuse, the new acquaintance said, "Well, there's a man ill at my house, and I think he's one of your people, and as I happen to be in town I thought I should tell you." Father Stafford then asked if the sick man expressed a wish to see him or any other priest, when the man on the street said, "No," and repeated, "but as I happened to be in town—" Father Stafford then asked where he lived, and was informed that he lived about seven miles from Lindsay, after which the traveller walked away.

The morning was delightful, but although the good Father could not say he had a sick call, since no one sent for him, still he lost all heart in his exercise, and did not care to resume it. It did not take him long to decide that he must away, although reluctantly, since it was Saturday morning, and he had arranged to hear the Confessions of the country people at an early hour. Leaving the ninety-nine in the desert he ordered his vehicle, entered it, and drove to the wayside inn indicated by his informer. A woman appeared at the door and seemed rather surprised to see the priest, and to his question, "Is there anyone ill in your house?" she unhesitatingly answered, "No." "Well, is your husband in Lindsay to-day?" Father Stafford pursued. "Yes," she replied, and added, "But there is a man here, who is outside near the barn, as he did not go to work to-day. Perhaps you wish to see him." Father Stafford replied in the affirmative, and presently seeing the man coming from near the corner of the house, he went forward to meet him, saluted him, and asked about his condition. The poor fellow told the good Father that he was not actually ill, but as it was the first morning he had not felt well, he thought he had better not go to work as usual. Then the priest said, "You are a Catholic. Have you been to Church lately?" To the former indirect question he assented, but excused his non-attendance at church by explaining that he was employed on a train and the runs made did not admit of his attending to this religious duty of obligation. Then the priest asked him if he would like to go to Confession, since he had come from Lindsay expressly on the representation of his host. The sick man's face beamed with pleasure and he gladly consented, when the priest noticed a change in his appearance, and offered to help him to his room, for which he seemed really grateful. On getting to his room "Begin your Confession at once," the priest said, "there may be no time to lose," and immediately the penitent commenced the confession which was to be his last. After the poor man had finished, Father Stafford called the woman to tell her he thought the man was dying, and then he turned to the sick man and said, "Now, please tell me what good act you have done in your past life, that you have received such an extraordinary grace." The dying man humbly said, "O, Father, I have done nothing to merit it, but one thing I have done, I have always sent half my wages every month to my mother and two sisters who live in D— and will you please tell them about me." Before the priest left the house, the poor man had passed away, and we hope, received his reward. When this incident was related to Rev. Mother Teresa by one who had heard it from the Father's own lips, her eyes filled with tears, and she said, "The good priest! I am afraid we shall not have him long." And her words seemed prophetic, for the great, active man whom everyone thought to be in the prime of life was already silently entering into the dark valley. His people scarcely saw a change in the busy life, when in reality it had nearly ebbed out. On Sunday, the 5th of November, he gave Holy Communion to the Nuns at the Convent and afterwards gave instructions to the children in the Church before celebrating the Holy Sacrifice. when it was noticed he seemed to be enduring great physical suffering, and considerable anxiety was felt during the ensuing week, when his familiar form was no longer seen in his wonted place in the sanctuary or on the street, and on Saturday his curate had to give the unwelcome news to anxious enquirers that he was dying. His last desire seemed to be to see his Bishop, but when told that though His Lordship, Bishop Jamot, was actually on his way to Lindsay, he would not probably live to see him. "Then send in my curate at once to administer the Last Sacraments," said he, Rev. Father Keating, the curate, was at hand to do as he desired, and after having received the last absolution, the true Pastor lived a short time, then passed away quietly, after having distinctly uttered the words, "Lord, have mercy on the soul of Michael Stafford."

The sad announcement of his death was made on

188

FOUNDATION OF LINDSAY

Sunday, November 12th, '82, from the altar steps
where he had stood the previous Sunday, and exhorted
his people to remember the words he had addressed to
them which he seemed to feel were his parting injunc-
tions to those for whom he had laboured.   The
sorrow at his death was general, and loudly expressed
by Protestants as well as Catholics for he was acknowledged to have been a priest seldom equalled in
sacerdotal zeal for all that was good.   On that very
year he had fought a hard fight to have Marmion
removed from the prescribed literature for candidates
writing the departmental examinations and the
objectionable election was withdrawn.   His Grace
Archbishop Lynch, who had warmly approved of this
last as well as his other good works, His Lordship
Bishop Jamot, his Bishop as he styled him, whom he
had so longed to see, and numerous priests of his
acquaintance, crowded into Lindsay to attend his
funeral and show respect to his memory.   By order
of the Mayor the stores were closed while the funeral
was passing through the principal streets, and the
words spoken by His Grace Archbishop Lynch so
effectively over the remains seemed to voice the universal sentiment of sorrow, for the loss of a great
leader in the community.   This blow was keenly felt
by Rev. Mother Teresa, for had he not been the constant friend and counsellor of the Community in
Lindsay; but the work he was mainly instrumental in
establishing continued with ever increasing success,
for some years after his demise, until a great fire completely demolished the edifice he had erected with such
anxious care, on the 24th of April, '84, about two

o'clock in the afternoon a message came for Rev. Mother Teresa informing her that the Convent in Lindsay was on fire. On hearing that no person was injured Rev. Mother remained perfectly calm, advising all to pray. The morning after she with a companion went to Lindsay and the scene around the Convent was indeed desolate, for the main building was all burnt, the walls and chimneys only remaining. Sorrow was depicted on every countenance especially on the faces of those who had witnessed the devotion, the unceasing interest the late Father Stafford had shown in its erection, its efficiency and success. The building was the ornament of the town and was regarded as Father Stafford's monument, but what are earthly monuments?—was a thought that might have presented itself to every mind. More than fifty men worked all the previous night to save the extension part of the building and the laundry which they succeeded in doing. Bishop Jamot presented the Fire Brigade a hundred dollars in recognition of their efforts. Later a card of thanks appeared from him in the press, expressing his appreciation of the labours of the men. Protestants and Catholics vied with each other in showing kindness and proffering hospitality to the Nuns and children. At a meeting of the Trustees presided over by the Bishop great appreciation of the Nuns' influence was shown by the resolution to reopen the classes at any sacrifice; the Nuns were domiciled in the priest's house, and other accommodations were secured for the separate schools. On the very first alarm of the fire a Sister who had been ailing for some time was taken to the home of Mrs.

190

FOUNDATION OF LINDSAY

Keenan, formerly Miss McAuley, one of the first pupils of the Nuns when they opened their first boarding school in Toronto. Passionately devoted to her early teachers, she, with characteristic generosity, gave the two largest rooms in her home, one for a class room and one for a music room, until the Nuns should be temporarily settled in more commodious quarters. The invalid Sister was carefully nursed by the daughter of the house, and it is interesting to note that this young lady afterwards became a member of the Institute. When the news first reached Rev. Mother that the Convent was burning, she telegraphed the Nuns to come home at once, but when on visiting Lindsay, they represented that it would spoil the year's work of the pupils, and put them and their parents to much inconvenience, she allowed them to remain some time longer, she returning to Toronto with the sick Sister who lived only a short time after. Indeed, the Nuns remained until a new house was built in which they resided for a short time before they were finally recalled to Toronto, and it is a noteworthy fact that as the young lady who passed highest in the departmental examinations in Lindsay became a member of the Institute, so the two last boarders to leave the house, after having successfully passed the same examinations, found their way to the Institute, where they have laboured for years strenuously for the advancement of God's kingdom. At the time of the recall of the Nuns, neither Archbishop Lynch, nor Father Stafford, nor Rev. Mother Teresa was alive, but Lindsay is by no means of the past, for it has a conspicuous place in the halls of the Institute in

191

REV. MOTHER TERESA DEASE

Toronto, where diplomas for Degrees obtained from
two Universities are framed, and in the class rooms
of the east and west its abiding influence is felt. Thus
notwithstanding the saying of Shakespeare, the good
that men do is not interred with their bones, but lives
on forever.

The Bishop who took such a fatherly interest in the
Community at the time of the fire was none other
than the faithful friend, and former vicar of Archbishop Lynch in the city of Toronto in the early
seventies. A letter characteristic of his genuine appreciation of the Community and interest in its progress,
spiritual and temporal, is here appended as a fitting
close to the Lindsay mission:

BRACEBRIDGE, 25th December.

Dear Rev. Mother,—

I thank you from my heart for all your good wishes
and prayers for these happy times. I know that I
have the prayers of you and of your most fervent
Community. That thought is a great relief to me in
very many difficulties. I beg to assure you that most
cheerfully I reciprocate your good wishes. I pray
for you, I ask, these times when the Blessed Infant
Jesus is so generous to those who love Him, to give an
abundance of blessings to you all. I shall not forget
to pray that God may assist you in the important
changes which you contemplate. Indeed, Mother M.
will do well anywhere she is sent. Of course she will
do well in Lindsay, and the other Superiors will be
equally successful in other places. When I think of
your fervent Community it is like a balm to my mem-

ory. May God keep them always so. To remove the Novitiate to the Abbey will be another important change, and everything is done for the spiritual benefit of those young Novices who are so well disposed when they come and who fall into such good hands. I had arranged to start to-morrow for my visit to our new settlers in the direction of Lake Nipissing. But for that, snow and sleighing are wanted, and so far, we have nothing but mud in abundance. So to my great regret that journey will have to be postponed for another week. Well, the Will of God be done. But I long so much to go to see those poor people. I feel so happy amongst them.

Wishing you again a Happy Christmas and a happier New Year.

> I am, very respectfully,
> Yours faithfully in Our Lord,

> + JOHN FRANCIS, Bp. of Sarepta,
> Vicar Apostolic of North. Canada.

This shows no change of feeling in the Bishop of Peterboro' from the Vicar of Toronto, but like many of Rev. Mother Teresa's friends, he too had passed away, ere the closing chapters of Loretto in Lindsay.

CHAPTER XVIII

STRATFORD FOUNDATION, DR. KILROY. LETTERS.

A REQUEST for a branch of the Institute in the London diocese was made early in 1878 by Rt. Rev. John Walsh, D.D., through Rev. Dr. Kilroy, Pastor of Stratford. There was much in this request that appealed to Rev. Mother Teresa, besides the gaining of souls which was her first and last ambition, for was not His Lordship one of the first and best friends of the Community when Vicar at St. Mary's, Toronto? He had well known the trials and virtues of the first Sisters, and expected much from those who succeeded them, and it pleased him much to think that Dr. Kilroy was one with him in appreciation of the Loretto Nuns. Indeed, he was heard once to say that if ever he should have to find fault with the Community he should feel personally grieved, for from his long acquaintance with the Sisters he expected nothing but the practice of exalted virtue.

On the feast of the Assumption, Aug. 15th, 1878, under the protection of their Blessed Mother, a little colony was despatched to the Classic City. Mother Gonzaga Galvin accompanied the members of this mission of which Mother Evangelistic O'Sullivan was to be Superior. At Berlin they were met by Dr. Kilroy, who had come expressly from Stratford to meet the party and accompany the Religious to their new home. No untoward accident happened, and Stratford was reached without delay where carriages containing the very best Catholic families of the place met them at the station. At the head of these was a young lady, Miss Corcoran, afterwards destined to be a member of the Institute. The drive to the Convent took very little time, and Dr. Kilroy, after the ladies had entered, presented the keys to the Superior. All were charmed with the homelike appearance of the new abode; and the beautiful orchard and garden attached to the residence, and the homelike verandah were specially admired. The Corcoran family had vacated their home, "Villa Rosa," for the summer, and here the Religious were most hospitably entertained by the eldest daughter of the house until the Chapel was arranged and everything in the Convent was in perfect readiness for occupancy. After the Chapel, always come the schools in Loretto, and so this first band had few spare moments until the first of September, but were busy making preparations for the opening of the Academy and separate schools. The house, although considered very spacious for a private residence, was not deemed large enough to receive boarders, and so the Day Academy opened with a very satisfactory attendance and the separate schools were crowded from the first. Nothing could exceed the kindness of the people of Stratford to the Nuns, and indeed it has never varied, through every vicissitude of Pastor and Prelate. The children were remarkably bright and the friendly rivalry between them and those of the Royal City in passing examinations has been well sustained. Dr. Kilroy always insisted that his school was at the head, but others were perfectly free to

195

their respective opinions, and so this harmless rivalry never caused a ripple on the Genesareth of religious life. When in the lapse of time the numbers of the Academy greatly increased, a new Chapel and a large wing were erected, and the Doctor's Feast day was one of great celebration for the children. How truly he loved them all, the Nuns who taught in his schools can testify, and happy are the recollections of the day when the first reception was given to His Lordship Bishop Walsh by the pupils of Stratford trained by the Loretto Nuns. Every word of encouragement the children received from the Prelate gladdened the heart of Dr. Kilroy and his beaming countenance gave ready response. The following letter will show in what esteem Rev. Mother Teresa was held by the Bishop of London, and how deeply appreciative he was of her zeal for the beauty of the House of the Lord:

BISHOP'S PALACE, LONDON, ONT.

Dear Rev. Mother,—

Although I have received no notification to that effect I am satisfied that you are the donor of the beautiful banner of the Blessed Virgin that has just arrived from Toronto. I need not say how deeply grateful I am, for this additional proof of your constant friendship, and kindly interest in my work. God, for Whose greater honour you do these things, will, I am sure, abundantly reward you. The banner is indeed a work of art, a real gem. On the day of the Dedication it will be borne at the head of the procession, and afterwards it will be hung from a granite pillar opposite the throne in the sanctuary. I shall

not fail to remember the giver in my poor prayers. I
ask you to pray that God may favour us with a clear
fine day on the 28th, and that He may give me the
grace and strength to do my duty in a nmanner worthy
of the episcopal office.

With kindest wishes for the happiness of you and
your Community in the here and hereafter, I am,

Faithfully yours,

+ JOHN WALSH,
Bishop of London.

REV. M. TERESA,
Superior of Loretto Community,
Toronto.

Perhaps one of the greatest gifts of God to poor
humanity is sympathy, and this Rev. Mother Teresa
possessed in a high degree. Though always calm and
unruffled exteriorly, she possessed the greatest depth
of feeling and could rejoice with those who were joyful and grieve with those in sorrow. Not that there
was ever much manifestation of her sentiments; but
all her spiritual children knew that there was no trial
or struggle of theirs in which she had not a part. A
single word or even look would often speak volumes
as to the depth of her sympathy, and no one ever
doubted the genuineness of it. Then, too, she had the
happy faculty of making each one believe that the
consideration shown to another was that other's
peculiar right, so there was never a jar, although of
course faults had to be corrected and preferences manifested and exigencies met as occasion required. The
following letter will show how intimately she was

acquainted with the peculiar trials of each member, for although addressed to one individual it may safely be taken as a type of her correspondence, and in the cherished long ago hundreds of such letters might be produced.

LORETTO ABBEY,
TORONTO, Oct. 27th, 1878.

My Dearest Sister M.M.,—

I received your letter with great pleasure. I am distressed lest the work be greater than your strength is equal to, but I am consoled and rejoiced to see your zeal and generosity. God will amply reward both if you are generous, God is munificent and will grant the fondest wishes of your heart. Write to me often, and tell me how you are getting on in every respect. Pray that God's Will may be done in us all, and that we may attain the end of our creation, so as to obtain a high degree of glory. St. Teresa calls this life "un souffle" and is it not? In a little time the labour will be over but the reward will last forever, not only what we merit for ourselves, but also what we shall have procured by our virtue and sufferings for those who are dear to us. Write me even a card when you have not time to fill a letter. I shall long to hear from you. I shall pray for your intentions in the Novena of All Saints.

With very much love,
Yours affectionately in C. J.,
M. J. TERESA.

This far reaching sympathy was the keynote of her success. On one occasion in the very early days the Portress remarked to her, that a poor woman at the door was shivering with cold. She immediately removed from her person a warm woollen garment which had been given her as a protection against the cold draughts of the badly heated house, and handed it to the Portress to give the poor sufferer, without uttering a single word, and making a gesture at the same time that there was to be no mention of the matter. Mental suffering, her quick perception noted without effort, and her attempts to relieve the victim of it were generally crowned with success. It has been said that when she visited the different branch houses, any little trouble that might have existed vanished with her presence. In such matters she was singularly clear sighted, and could at once detect whether the trouble was real or imaginary. Of course, she had sometimes to remonstrate, and her reasoning, clear as a lawyer's, never failed to convince those who knew that she had only their best interests at heart, and the greater glory of God. She was highly appreciative of good in others, secular or religious, and what carried the greatest balm to an afflicted heart was, that she meant exactly what she said. To one of the Religious who had lost her mother, she wrote as follows: "Blessed are the dead who die in the Lord."

My Dearest M.M.,—

Your beloved Mother has justly merited the title of Blessed, since we cannot doubt that she died in the love and friendship of God. What a subject of consolation for you all, in your great, great trial to think of the rich reward awaiting the well spent life, and the many virtues of your dear Mamma, for in fact, what virtue was there which she did not possess? I often thought, after an interview with her, that she always said and did just the right thing. Truly may you be thankful to God for having given such a Mother to show the way to Heaven to you, and indeed for having spared her to you so long. I prayed often for her, and this morning I prayed to her as well.

With much sympathetic love, I am,

Ever affectionately in C. J.,

M. J. TERESA.

When she heard of a lady in the world spiritually inclined, it gave her real pleasure, especially if the person was known to acquit herself faithfully of her duty to her family. When a Religious remarked that her mother often caused some portion of the Lives of the Saints to be read at home while they were dining, she immediately remarked, "What a holy soul! and with such a large family to care for. No wonder God has blessed her." On one occasion when returning from a very pleasant visit to Stratford, she and her companion noticed a poor child eyeing them very closely, and as the little waif seemed to be alone, Rev. Mother Teresa remarked to her companion, that she would like to know where the child was going and what she intended to do, as she seemed to be quite alone. They called the little creature to them and on questioning her found out that she was going to Toronto, and her destination was an aunt's house there, of the street and number of which she seemed to have only a hazy recollection. "But it will be night when we reach Toronto," Rev. Mother said. "Do you expect anyone to meet you?" The child answered, "No," and immediately Rev. Mother said that Providence had brought her to their notice so that they might look after her until she was safely sheltered. The Abbey carriage met them at the station, and Rev. Mother and her companion took the child with them and drove for over two hours until they finally located her destination, and left her in safety. Many fears were entertained at the Abbey by those who remained up to wait for the Religious, when neither the carriage nor the Nuns arrived two hours after the time the train was due. Nor did they hear that night the cause of the delay, for it was the time of silence, and Rev. Mother went to her cell without a word. Her companion explained the reason of the long drive the day after, but Rev. Mother never mentioned the matter.

There had been much steady growth in this portion of God's garden, and rich foliage bordered the Stratford field of labour, so after some time had passed Rev. Mother was anxiously looking for fruit, nor had she long to wait. She often remarked that the children of those in any mission who had come forward to lend a helping hand to the Religious in their first struggle, invariably became Religious, and the children of Stratford were no exception to this rule. Mrs. Corcoran, although away with her family at a summer resort, had arranged to place her beautiful residence at the Nuns' disposal as we have seen, leaving her eldest daughter in charge to receive them. Indeed, to this day her name is gratefully remembered by the Stratford Community, and the reward of her generosity was not long delayed, for her eldest daughter became the first Postulant from Stratford, and although she had not the satisfaction of witnessing the ceremony of the reception of her cherished child, many thoughts on the day of the Clothing were directed to the generous benefactress of the early Stratford mission. Many other daughters of the town on the Avon followed, and to-day a fair colony represents the Classic City, in the ever increasing band of Mother Teresa's daughters.

How careful she was of the perfection and salvation of each soul entrusted to her care was evidenced by every word she ever spoke and every line she ever wrote, and indeed, her letters are full of solicitude for the health of body and soul of each member, and contain little else. She writes to one, who in leaving the world had left much.

LORETTO ABBEY,
TORONTO (Undated).

My Dear M.M.,—

Your dear Mamma and Emily R. came to the Abbey. I was really happy to see both. They looked well, and were in good spirits. I hope you are faithful to all your good resolutions. . . . Keep silence, and it will keep you from almost every serious fault. I saw a remark from Nouet, "We need the grace of God to speak well." Can we expect it when we speak at a time when our rule forbids us to speak? I feel sure you will keep the rule that will ensure your perfection. I mean the rule of silence. We are praying for dear M.M.M. With love to all,

Yours fondly in C. J.,
202   M. J. TERESA.

To another she writes on the score of health:

LORETTO ABBEY,
TORONTO, 16th August.

My Dear S.M.M.,—

I think you would have a chance of getting better if you gave up the painting completely and had nothing whatever to do in that line. I shall arrange this with M.M.M. Perhaps you might still teach drawing, but we shall see. I am very sure that the health of your soul gives you very much more concern than the bodily ailments from which you suffer so much. It would indeed be sad were it otherwise, which it is not, thank God. S.M.A. will return to Toronto very soon, so the circle of Saints in Hamilton is narrowing, or I should have said, growing less. Poor S.M.A. had not much benefit from her change of air. I should like her to have another trip on the water which I may be able to manage soon. S.M.D. and she would enjoy a few days at the Falls I am sure.

Love to all,

Yours fondly in J. C.,

M. J. TERESA.

The different communities of Loretto Nuns scattered over the Convents in Ontario made one very compact family, and at the time Stratford was the youngest member, but from far outside the Province of Ontario for a long time, requests had been coming to the Foundress for filiations. Some of these appealed very strongly to her, but she would never consent to a foundation which would have to be severed from the parent house as was stipulated in some cases. Then, again, she preferred strengthening the houses already founded, before spreading the Institute over distant fields, knowing that expansion would come in the due order of time. How well and wisely she calculated, recent events have shown. But she was truly of an apostolic nature, and could never hear of great things being done for God, without expressing a wish that an opportunity might be given her to show the zeal for the Father's house that consumed her. She was singularly appreciative of the good she saw in other communities. When visiting some of her houses she occasionally had to pass a night in convents not of her order, and then she always remarked some particular virtue which she observed in the Religious. In one house it was silence. She said the whole Community rose in a body, and as she was making her own preparation to receive Our Lord she did not hear a sound, although the Religious had all left their places in the choir and approached the altar rail. In another it was poverty and industry; after one visit she explained to the sacristan, how beautifully and decoratively she had seen flower pots covered with stiff paper, and she brought a sample home with her; but when she saw an elegant church she was in an ecstasy of delight that somewhere someone had a proper idea of what was due to the Majesty of God in His temples, but her constant theme and exhortation to the Nuns was to form in the hearts of the children temples where the Holy Ghost might be pleased to dwell. She kept in touch with each Religious in all of her houses, and the fragments of letters that remain

204

are redolent of the beautiful faith that was the main-spring of her whole life. Perhaps she was in her happiest vein when writing festal letters, and on the feasts of the Patron Saints of the Nuns she always found some means of conveying to them her felicitations either by writing to themselves as in some cases, or by conveying her kindly sentiments to them in her letters to others. Every Sister felt that when the Martyrology was read in the Refectory and her Patron Saint was announced, a prayer went up for her to the great White Throne from a soul in the state of grace, who was never unmindful of the spiritual well being of those who looked up to her. The following is a type of her correspondence of this kind:

LORETTO ABBEY,
TORONTO, June 19th.

My Dearest M.M.,—

I wish you a most happy feast and in plenitude the virtues of your most holy patron. Busy as all or mostly all are here, they have time to think of you, and I am sure to pray for you and yours,—the sharers of your toils. I must ask our dear holy Sister Juliana to pray very specially for you on the 21st though I am sure she would not forget to do so, she is so kind and charitable, and grateful to every member of the Community that she had anything to do with. She is wasting slowly. I returned from Belleville yesterday and left everyone pretty well except M.N. who suffers from sleeplessness very much. Dear M.S. is strong and well. D. G., Mgr. Farrelly has gone to Kingston to prepare the way for His Lordship who is expected on the 25th of this month. The reception will be very grand, fully worthy of the strong faith of the truly Catholic people of Kingston. I am sure Sister A. is glad to hear of the profession of her sister. Tell her B. is well and very good. Our Distribution will be on the 25th. I like your card of invitation to the closing exercises. Give my love to all the dear Nuns. You will be well and affectionately remembered by all here to-morrow. Many happy and holy returns of your feast.

Yours fondly in J. C.,

M. J. TERESA.

Even in her relations with her family which were doubly sacred, the bond of religion was not second to the bond of nature, for we find that on leaving Fermoy with the Nun who accompanied her, and the last good bye was said by the two Sisters, who, sisters of the same Community as well as sisters by nature, were such instruments for the advancement of God's glory in Ireland and America, looking into each others' faces and feeling that in all probability this was their last meeting on earth—which it really was—not a word was spoken, but simultaneously each drew her rosary from her girdle, and presented it to the other. Precious memento of a truly religious parting which each carried to her death, until she was introduced at the heavenly court by her Spouse to the Queen, in the land where partings are no more.

CHAPTER XIX

REV. MOTHER TERESA'S LAST FOUNDA-
TION, JOLIET.

MANY urgent appeals came to Rev. Mother Teresa to extend her sphere of influence beyond Canada as before mentioned, and indeed, nothing would have pleased her better, but she felt an obligation to the country that had first received her and her companions, and until she could feel that the houses in this allotted province were well supplied with teachers, she would not consider any filiation in the United States, much as her heart desired to work in that generous land of progress. However, in 1880, an invitation came from a quarter by no means more desirable than several others which she had previously refused, but as the condition of the Novitiate showed that a branch might be established without weakening the parent tree, she felt that it was the Will of God she should accept the cultivation of this portion of the Lord's vineyard.

An opening in the States meant very little of a new departure, for the profession of teaching is not so different in English speaking countries as might be imagined, from the different systems of government, and God and souls are the same the world over. This, Rev. Mother's experience had taught her, and with the ever abiding faith so marked in her whole career, she commenced the work which was destined to be felt in the not distant future. When Montalembert visited

England, accompanied by his bride—his most ardent expectations fully realized, he called on a literary friend, not a Catholic, who remarked that he envied not the great Frenchman the prosperity that had come to him, but the faith that seemed to be the guiding star of his life. So, with the deep religious convictions that formed Rev. Mother Teresa's most valuable asset, she set out to Joliet, Illinois, on Tuesday, the 29th of August, 1880, to commence what has proved to be a very flourishing mission. Rev. Father Power, the Pastor, had known the Loretto Nuns in Hamilton, and as the little convent which had been previously occupied by the Sisters of the Holy Cross was entirely devoid of furniture, Rev. Mother and her companions, M. Aloysius Gonzaga, M. Dosithea and Sr. Lidwina, were obliged to accept the hospitality of Rev. Father Power for the week. Great was the good Pastor's surprise to find they had come to found a mission almost penniless, for having seen their convents in Canada and having known nothing of the poverty of their foundations, he half expected they would commence to build immediately an edifice similar to some of those convents of theirs he had seen in other places. Rev. Mother, on the other hand, was a little disappointed that somewhat better accommodation had not been provided for the Nuns, and on her homeward journey, as she stopped at one of the houses of the order, and looked over the surrounding country she pointed to a small house in the middle of an uncultivated field, and with the thought present with her of the Sisters she had just left, she broke silence, and tears gathered in her eyes as she said, "In a place something

208

like that I left the Nuns." On Sept. 8th, the feast of
Our Lady's Nativity, the little band that she had left
in Illinois took possession of their Nazareth. On the
same day the Academy was opened with only eight
pupils in attendance.

A few days before the parochial school was opened
in the basement of St. Patrick's church. Twenty-five
children, boys and girls, presented themselves and this
number daily increased. On Sept. 9th the arrival of
two Nuns, a music teacher and a class teacher, from
Canada, was hailed with delight by the heroic little
band, who had resolved to plant the seeds of virtue in
the souls of the children God had sent to them. For
persons who live their lives in the shadow of the
sanctuary, there is a strange feeling if ever they find
themselves in a house where the Tabernacle is unten-
anted. So the Nuns set to work to prepare a place as
suitable as their hands and means could make it, for
the reception of the Divine Guest, and on the Octave
of the Nativity of Our Blessed Lady their kind Pastor, Father Power, consoled them by bringing into
their midst the Blessed Sacrament. Then, after the
hard day's work in the schools, there was the visit to
our Divine Lord and the comfort that His abiding
Presence brings. Sister Lidwina, who has long since
gone to Heaven, was indefatigable in trying to give a
homelike appearance to the badly furnished small
rooms, and after four o'clock each day, she had many
assistants. For as the numbers in the schools increased, so did the number in the Community, and
the 17th of September was again marked by fresh
arrivals from Canada. Rev. Mother Teresa showed

the greatest consideration to those going on what was then deemed a very distant mission, and personally saw to what was provided for them on their journey. Indeed, the gift of sympathy so often referred to caused tears to come to her eyes in speaking of some hardships endured by these absent children, but at recreation those dear missioners themselves enjoyed many a laugh over the discomfort and contrivances in their new home, and poverty, which is often the lot of the Religious of the Institute in imposing edifices, was quite conspicuous in the sleeping apartments and refectory of the poor little convent.

On the feast of St. Stanislaus, Benediction of the Blessed Sacrament was given for the first time in the little Chapel by the Pastor. How piously the Nuns assisted thereat, and how sincerely they thanked God for this great privilege which they had missed for some time, may be gleaned from the annals of the West. The feasts of Our Lady and of some Patron Saints seem to have been red letter days in their lives, for blessings spiritual or temporal appear to have come to them on these festivals in a more marked way than at other times. They needed all the encouragement they received for the weather became unusually cold for this early season, and the Community suffered from its effects, so that even the necessaries of life were wanting until they found that their credit was something they might draw on. The winter of 1880, according to old settlers, was more severe than any experienced for twenty-five years. During part of that season the people were obliged to have recourse to ladders for egress from the second story of their houses, owing to the great snowdrifts. Then followed the protracted autumn during which the inhabitants might have deluded themselves that they were living in a modern Venice, as they were compelled to use boats in going from one house to another, particularly in the lower parts of the city.

There was much to discourage the young Community this first year of its existence under the Stars and Stripes, for disappointments followed one another in rapid succession. It has often been noted that the darkest hour precedes the dawn, and a rosy one, according to the Community point of view, was at hand. The first Mass in the little home was celebrated, the first Benediction of the Blessed Sacrament given in the little Chapel, and in the usual order of Loretto, the first examination was held on the 16th of December in the presence of Rev. Fathers Power, Burke and Dunne. The Pastor and attendant priests marvelled at the progress made by the pupils in such a short time, and though looking only for the "well done" of the Master, it was a solace to the strangers in a strange land, to know that their work for souls was appreciated by those who had the best right to know what was being done for the education of the little ones of Christ. Then, as usual, followed the Triduum in preparation for the feast of the Nativity, and truly no greeting gladdened more the heart of Rev. Mother Teresa on the Blessed Morn than that which came from her children of the far West. How heartily she rejoiced with them that the opening struggle was over, and that they were enjoying the "come-apart" with the Divine Master. Of the great

211

grace of vocation to work for God anywhere she was fully sensible, and one of her most beautiful exhortations to the Religious was on "Fidelity to Our Vocation." She said, "How grateful we should be to God for our vocation for being chosen to be of God's elect to continue the work of the Apostles. What merit did God see in us that He should have chosen us? Could He have seen any? We are to do more for God, greater things for God than seculars; we are the body guard of Jesus, we are nearer to Him than others, we are to gain conquests for God, to establish His reign in hearts that do not know Him. We are to fight against the world, the flesh and the devil and we are sure of victory. Jesus tells us, He will not ask us to do anything of which He has not given us an example. We wear His livery to appear like unto Him, and declare to all our mission. How honoured we should feel to labour and suffer for God, even if we should receive no other reward than the privilege of doing so. If we would even think of the great evil we shall escape by being of the elect, namely, freedom from the company of the reprobate, from the pain of loss, from hell. We should often reflect on the joys of Heaven and on the pains of hell. The latter, some say, ought never to be mentioned to Religious; again others say, it is necessary to reflect on them, as the love of God is not always powerful enough to keep us faithful. Eye hath not seen nor ear heard the joys of Heaven, yet we can form a faint idea of them just as we can form some idea of hell. Saint Francis Borgia said he warmed himself daily at the gates of hell, and one of the preludes to his

212

meditation was to imagine himself in hell under the feet of Lucifer; this thought strengthened him to bear any suffering during the day. We should ever have our Model before us and consider how He would perform each action. How He would pray, walk, act on such an occasion, how condescending and kind He would be to all. We should aim at perfection in all things, we should be models that those committed to our care might safely copy. We owe this to the Institute. Any defect in one spoils the beauty of the whole. We are each of us parts of the great edifice of the Institute. If the architect in examining a building sees a stone out of line, and rough, he will say at once, "Take it out, it is not suitable. Take it away." In the same manner, when the great Architect, God Himself, surveys His building He will say, "That stone spoils its beauty. Let it be taken out." Let us not give Him reason to say anything similar of us. "I have loved, O Lord, the beauty of Thy House, and the place where Thy glory dwelleth. Obedience is the mortar which keeps each stone in its place. We are to learn humility from our Lord. Let us think of the day of our profession when we told God Himself that we preferred humiliations and contempt in the House of God rather than to dwell in the habitation of sinners. We were in earnest then. Let us not mock God, but receive joyfully what we came to seek."

On Christmas the Reverend Pastor presented a very valuable silver service to the little struggling Community which act of generosity in their poverty-stricken circumstances evoked warm expressions of gratitude for the generosity of the donor, but the smile of the Master for Whom they toiled was to be soon in evidence; for the children whom they had been instructing through that memorable winter in preparation for their first Holy Communion were bidden to approach the altar and receive the Bread of Life on May the 8th. Memorable day in the annals of the Institute. How many First Communion classes numbering hundreds have since approached the altars of St. Patrick's and St. Mary's church, as well as that of the Sacred Heart; and how many streams of benediction have flowed to children and parents from the life-giving Sacrament there received?

On May the 18th, Rev. Mother Teresa, accompanied by Mother M. Ignatia, visited her new filiation and remained five days with her most distant missioners. Indescribable, the annalist says, was the delight of her children of the far West at having the pious Foundress again in their midst. Her very presence on this occasion was felt to be cheery, and the account of all that had been done and suffered for souls was to her an inspiration. On May 14th Archbishop Feehan visited Joliet, and arranged with the Pastors what he decided would be for the benefit of the children of the city, that the Community should move from St. Patrick's to St. Mary's parish, where the population was larger, and a Religious Community needed. Rev. Father Burke, the Pastor, (present Bishop of St. Joseph's, Missouri) was instructed to rent a house until such a time as a convent could be built, the rent to be paid by the Pastor. Although Rev. Father Burke must have been greatly embarrassed by the removal of the

Nuns to his parish, just after the erection of his very beautiful church, he received them with the utmost cordiality, and with the magnanimity and generosity which they found to be truly characteristic of his nature. From the advent of the Nuns to his parish, until his elevation to the Bishopric of Cheyenne, his solicitude for the temporal and spiritual welfare of the Community was unceasing. Indeed, to the present time, his name is held in blissful remembrance by those Nuns who more directly experienced his kindness as well as by the rest of the Community who had heard of his benefactions. In the old days of his pastorate his visits to the school and Community were looked forward to with the greatest pleasure, and after his appointment to an Episcopal See, it was a matter of rejoicing for all, that the first to greet the newly appointed Shepherd were the Religious and pupils of Loretto Abbey, Toronto, as His Lordship was travelling in Canada when the Bulls reached him, and an impromptu entertainment at the Mother House of Loretto was his second surprise.

On July the 26th, the first Mass was said in the Cass St. house, Joliet, and immediately after the blessing of the new convent followed. On September 1st, 1881, Archbishop Feehan again visited Joliet and preached the sermon at High Mass, when he highly recommended aiding the Community. The Franciscan Fathers, who resided in a distant part of the city, were always willing to render spiritual service when solicited and very kind mention is made of the first Retreat preached by Rev. F. Gerhardt, O.S.F., to the pioneer members. History repeats itself, and three flourishing schools established in Joliet have a record not differing very greatly from the sister Institutions of Loretto in Canada, only perhaps the numbers increased more rapidly in the West, for we find ere the memorable year of '81 had waned, the Academy counted its pupils by the hundreds and the Nuns had to give up their cells and convert class rooms into dormitories for the night, and before the bell rang for morning meditation, had to leave in perfect order shining, well-aired class rooms for the pupils. New Sisters arrived from Canada to aid in the work, and the only solution of the problem of housing was to build a new convent. The same refectory served both for Nuns and children, and here, too, poverty was conspicuous not only in the time spent at meals but in the fare of the Religious. The generous Pastor left nothing undone for the furtherance of the Nuns' interests and for the encouragement of the little ones of his flock; and a gold medal which he offered for competition was more eagerly contested for by the pupils, more because of the donor than because of its intrinsic value or the educational status which it gave to the winner. The children were all one in their desire to please the good priest in every respect, and as the years have gone by, his early expectations for them have been very happily realized.

September the 26th of that eventful year, brought a guest, to whose coming more than ordinary importance was attached by members of the Joliet Community, for he was no less a person than the first faithful friend of early days in Canada, Most Rev. Archbishop Lynch of Toronto. He was accompanied by his devoted vicar, Rev. Father McCann, then a young priest, Chancellor of the Diocese. His Grace was delighted with what he saw of the progress of the schools and Community, and playfully suggested the erection of a tent on the grounds to serve for class rooms, until such time as a new convent could be built.

On August 16th, 1883, the Nuns moved into the spacious convent known as St. Mary's Academy, to which additions have since been made, and which still lacks space for the ever increasing number of students. The dedication of the convent by Most Rev. Archbishop Feehan followed its completion on the 15th of August, and on the same day, His Grace administered Confirmation to two hundred of the pupils. The generosity of the Pastor was again in evidence in the furnishing of the new Chapel, and the ladies vied with one another in presenting whatever was deemed useful or necessary for the house. Truly the record of the first house in the United States keeps in very close parallelism with the Canadian foundations, for the first pupil who obtained a Teacher's Certificate from the Superintendent of Schools of Joliet, was the first to enter the Novitiate of the Mother House, and has happily celebrated her silver jubilee in the Divine service. This was the mark of progress for which Rev. Mother was always on the lookout, which seemed to give her work the special seal of God's approbation, which alone she coveted. Of course, she saw only the first fruits of this, her last mission, but the hope remains with her children that in Heaven she is aware of the good effected in the souls of the many who claim Loretto for their Alma Mater.

REV. MOTHER TERESA DEASE

The first band of Graduates numbering eight went out from Joliet in 1886, and the pleasure afforded to the Community by the realization of their desires for the advancement and betterment of their young charges, was participated in by the Mother who had followed them in thought through the trying years that led up to success. She was unwearied in hearing of their piety at prayer, and their devotion to the Blessed Virgin during the month of May shown by them in the acts of virtue practiced under the eyes of their Mistresses, and in their zeal for decorating Our Lady's altar, and taking part in the processions in her honour, and other traits of devotedness peculiar to Loretto's children. Had she lived to attend the first meeting of the Alumnae of this same Loretto, nothing would have pleased her better, perhaps, than hearing the President solemnly remind her companions, that as in the well remembered school days at Loretto Academy, night prayers were said before tea on evenings when entertainments were given by the pupils, lest any impediment should prevent the recital of them after, so on that auspicious occasion the custom was to be observed with old time fervour.

Among the many visitors to the celebration of the Silver Jubilee at which this reunion took place, was their first Mistress, Mother M. Dosithea, who could surely look with pardonable pride on these exemplars of her inculcated principles, and they, in turn, took the greatest delight in recalling the practices of early school days. Many were among them who remembered the gracious presence of Rev. Mother Teresa on her visits to their class rooms, and her words of kindly advice and encouragement, and they were good enough to remark that they prized her acquaintance as a privilege, not shared in by those who had come later, and a loss to them, which although not felt, having never known her, not lightly to be estimated. Indeed, seeing her only at intervals as the pupils of the distant convents did, it is possible that a too favourable impression of her sanctity might have been made on casual observers, but the fact remains, that to those who were always nearest her person, the charm of her holiness seemed most evident. Her assistant in these later years and afterwards her successor, Rev. M. Ignatia, was never weary of repeating, that from the day she entered the boarding school until the last sad days came, she could never see the smallest deviation from the aspiration to religious perfection which claimed her highest admiration. Indeed, it was a source of unalloyed pleasure to the Mistress of Novices to hear some of her spiritual daughters say, that they observed some hitherto unnoticed virtue in the holy Foundress, which occasion or necessity revealed. When on her visitation to the missions, nothing of good escaped her notice, and after her return from the different convents the Religious of the Abbey were sure to hear what edified or pleased her most in the other filiations.

On her return from Joliet on one occasion she remarked the sincere piety of the children in the Chapel and the reverence of the younger children at their prayers, and walking in the corridors when the doors of the class rooms were open in the sultry summer, she saw that every child in each room, kneeling at her desk, held her beads in her hand while answering the rosary. This happened on the day of her arrival at the Academy, and in relating the circumstances she added, "And there was such a multitude of them." "There's M.M.'s training! She gets the children *to do* what is right." And this was what really appealed to her spiritual sense, that the pupils were not merely taught or advised in a right way, but that they did what was right. It were easy to surmise that the Mistresses in charge of the schools of the Mother House did not wait for many rotations of the earth to see whether each child had her chaplet in hand at the signal for "Beads," and in this connection it might be said that she was equally acute in her sense of observation of anything in which there was a taint of evil.

In one of the Academies a Sister who was most anxious to have Rev. Mother's opinion of the method of teaching she pursued in her class, invited her specially one morning to hear a lesson in rhetoric. The pupils were aware that Rev. Mother was expected, and were told by their Instructress that to show the thoroughness of their understanding of the subject they were to seek out sentences for scansion from any books they might have in their possession, and without showing them to her, write them on the board and give the name of the verse, and mark out the feet. These sentences or lines were not to be familiar or easy or from the best known works. The second young lady who went to the blackboard wrote her sentence and began to explain, when Rev. Mother asked the Religious presiding at the class, from what work the extract was taken. The Religious explained that these lines were not conned under her supervision but were "home work" prepared for a test of thoroughness. Rev. Mother smiled very sweetly at the young lady who had taken such pains to acquit herself creditably at the test, and asked her to bring her the work from which she had taken the lines as she did not remember the setting. The child immediately went to her desk and brought forth a prose work, at the heading of one of the chapters of which was the single stanza which she had appropriated. Rev. Mother looked at the book and remarked she did not think it belonged to the Convent Library. The young lady assured her she had brought it from home the previous Sunday, but had not yet obtained permission to read it. She was kindly advised to abstain from the intellectual feast as the author was well known to lean to infidelity, which Rev. Mother gleaned from perusing the few lines ere she had any knowledge of their source. Her care in the matter of reading and the books provided for the pupils was constant and assiduous as the following letter will show:

LORETTO ABBEY, TORONTO.

My Dearest S.M.M.,—

I think the best way to arrange about the First Communion is to have an understanding with S.M. and enter into her views. God's blessing will attend the wish to maintain peace. It is likely from what I hear that poor S.M. will not be able to do much about the C. class. It is a pleasure to me to hear from you and to know that you have the advantage of having such beautiful sermons, beautiful in every sense. O, how grateful we should be for the pure and holy doctrine of Catholicity. The reason I make this remark now is, that I have been looking over books presented to the Library before allowing them placed there. Some of them, beautifully written, have a taint of heresy which renders them odious, so I sent them off, without the knowledge, of course, of the donor. Dearest S. M., I hope you will spend a holy, happy Easter and be rejoiced by good news from home, the pleasing tidings that your dear papa and all are well and happy. Once again wishing you and all a Happy Easter.

Yours fondly in J. C.,

M. J. TERESA.

CHAPTER XX

REV. MOTHER TERESA'S TRIALS, SACRI-FICES AND ZEAL.

THE trials of all Christian as well as other soldiers, come in connection with their work, and glancing over the open pages of the foundations, and workings of the establishments which owed their existence in a secondary way to Rev. Mother Teresa, we find the mark of the Cross everywhere. It is the cross which brings a blessing and without which no foundation will prosper. The years following the foundation of her last establishment, St. Mary's Academy, Joliet, were no exception to those preceding, and although the abundant harvest compensated for many a weary hour, still the anxiety that is ever attendant on a great enterprise was keenly felt as the years went on. The first great loss to the Institute of those who had been its unfailing friends was Rev. Michael Stafford, and as frequently happens this event was the forerunner of many bereavements which followed in due time and place. To each and all the holy Foundress bowed in meek resignation, and her spirit of silence and prayer became, if possible, more marked. Her grateful nature could never be unmindful of a kindness done to any of her communities, and the appreciation of their labours in different spheres of action was as balm to her heart. On the 2nd of October, following the demise of the lamented priest, the new wing of the Abbey containing the Chapel was blessed by Archbishop Lynch, and although as before mentioned this building did not afford her all the satisfaction she had anticipated, on account of her disappointment in the Chapel, still it gave accommodation to the ever increasing number of boarders, and thus relieved her of much anxious care. About this time two deaths, precious in the sight of God, gave her much consolation, although one of them, that of a Religious, was, perhaps, humanly speaking, a most severe loss to the Institute. But when the fiat came, and no one could be found who ever saw the rare soul during her life in religion commit even an imperfection, Rev. Mother, though mourning in her human heart, thanked God that the heights were gained and that the Institute gave back to the Creator one who had spent her earthly term in pleasing Him.

The other was that of a secular, a former pupil, whose mother was converted on her marriage to a Catholic, and did not receive as much instruction as was necessary in her case. The daughter of this lady after leaving the convent, living in a Protestant atmosphere, had been neglectful of her religious duties, and had almost entirely lost her faith, when gradually her strength failed her and the weariness that lay upon her made her long for change of scene. The case was reported to Rev. Mother Teresa who inquired particularly into her condition, and invited her to come to Loretto, Bond St., to recuperate. The hectic flush of her cheek and her extreme attenuation showed her to be in the last stage of consumption, but of this she did not dream at first, and gradually the Religious reminded her of the precarious state of her health and the certainty of her having to answer the Master's summons in the near future. But still there seemed no awakening; while making a friendly call at the Convent Bishop O'Mahoney was apprised of her state and immediately expressed a wish to see her. For the first time she seemed to realize her unpreparedness and to express a wish to make her peace with God. Very fervent prayers were offered before the throne of the Most High that God might, in His great mercy, enlighten her. So she expressed a wish to see the Bishop again, and on his coming the day after, she told him she wanted to go to confession, but did not seem to think she was dying. After having heard her confession and given her absolution, the Prelate informed her she had only a few hours to live, which news she received in perfect peace, although a short time before no doctor could persuade her of her danger. On the 2nd of November, the feast of All Souls, she passed away without a struggle at half past five, and Mass was immediately celebrated for her in the Convent Chapel. Rev. Mother's gratitude for the mercy of God to the child who had for a long time given up the practice of her religion, was very visible in her countenance, indeed, in cases where she obtained great favours from the Most High, she was, as a rule, silent.

The shadow of the cross which was in evidence at the time of the Lindsay fire was not without its consolations, for we see that almost immediately after Rev. Mother's return to Toronto from Lindsay, a ceremony of the reception and profession of several members took place. The invalid, whom she had brought with her from Lindsay, seemed to rally for awhile, but on the feast of the Sacred Heart so great a change was noticed in her that she was anointed and received the Holy Viaticum for the first and last time on Sunday at ten o'clock. This Sister's great devotion was to the Blessed Sacrament, and often during the night when seized by a coughing spell she suffered greatly from thirst, but refrained from moistening her lips with a drop of water, in order not to lose Communion the following morning. She had drawn Wednesday for the day of her Communion of Reparation, and was most faithful to the observance of this practice, or rather the fulfilment of its obligation; and the First Friday of June had completed her Novena of First Fridays which was offered for two intentions, the grace of reception into the Institute of her sister, and a happy death for herself. The result of both intentions seemed to be realized, for her sister was received on the 28th of May, and her own great change commenced on the feast of the Sacred Heart, on which day her sufferings became most acute. When the Confessor was taking leave of her on Sunday evening, she asked him if he thought she was dying. He exhorted her to be ready to meet her Saviour at any moment and all night her aspiration was, "Jesus, my Spouse, come to me!" Her perfect love and confidence were most consoling to Rev. Mother and those around her, and these sentiments never left her. With her last breath, when her voice was gone, she still articulated faintly with her lips, "Jesus, my Spouse, come to me!" A few moments before her death, she renewed her Vows. This renewal she had made many times during the night and always with the greatest fervour. Her calm departure, without any evidence of struggle and her happy smile, showed that her Jesus had met her. Perhaps the chief characteristic of this good Sister Juliana, during life, was her willingness to suffer. She was often heard to say, "I love to suffer for you, my Jesus!" and in making her night offering she was wont to offer every spasm of pain during her long wakeful night. Until the last night of her life no one watched with her, she could not bear to let anyone lose her rest in remaining up with her. A Sister once entered the room and said she had obtained permission to keep vigil with her that night. She replied, "I am not at all lonely or afraid, I can speak to Our Lord while looking at the Crucifix," and turning very earnestly to the sister who had followed her into religion, she said, "You have no idea how well I can speak to Our Lord. I can speak to Him for hours. I would not wound His Sacred Heart by doubting." According to her faith was it done unto her.

The distribution of prizes had to follow the funeral ceremony very closely, as the day had been appointed the month previous; and it was remarked that no closing exercises were ever more entirely satisfactory than those which followed so nearly the death of the Saintly Sister. His Grace Archbishop Lynch, Bishop O'Mahoney, and nearly all the clergy of the diocese, with the Mayor of Toronto and the Speaker of the House of Commons, were present, and on that occasion the daughter of the proprietor of the "Irish Canadian" was awarded the Governor-General's medal for English Literature, and received the congratulations of her father's confrères of the press, which was very complimentary in its account of the entertainment. The faint gleam of sunshine for Rev. Mother Teresa did not last long, for in July her brother, in far away Australia, was stricken with his mortal illness, and from West Kempsey, Macleay, on the 5th of August, the following appreciation of her much loved brother was forwarded to her, "The demise of a true Catholic and thorough Irishman, Christopher John Nugent Dease, at Kempsey, Macleay River, on Friday, 25th July, 1884, caused wide regret through many parts of the colony, outside his own locality, where for over ten years he lavishly expended the resources of a cultured mind and a genial disposition. The late Mr. Dease belonged to a family, especially on the maternal side, which gave statesmen and warriors to the principal countries of Europe. The record of their fame may be found in the archives of France, Austria and Spain, while the Deases of Turbotstown, allied with the noble house of Fingal, have been amongst the most patriotic of the Irish gentry."

The subject of this appreciation was a man of infinite humour. His geniality was inexhaustible, while the experiences of the best society in many lands made him a brilliant raconteur. His mind was a treasury of exquisite anecdotes, but a better recommendation than all these was, that he was politically a loyal follower of the great O'Connell, breathing all that tribune's ardour of hope for the regeneration of his country and the full possession of liberty of

228

conscience. With all Mr. Dease's intensity of religious feeling, still he was amongst the most tolerant of mortals, a fact he demonstrated in the conduct of his journal, *The Macleay Herald*, in the columns of which he reflected the serene brightness of his mind and geniality of his disposition. Notwithstanding physical disabilities, consequent on a fall from his horse some twelve years before, he became a moving spirit and a shining light on both banks of the Macleay; and it is to his enlightened zeal the public are mainly indebted for the reformatory prison and promised harbour of refuge at Trial Bay. Those who knew him best are not likely to neglect the profound expression of sympathy towards those who are bereaved by his death, to wit, his wife and children. From the fullness of the heart thousands of his co-religionists have already besought the Father of Mercy to shed perpetual light upon his soul.

The love of her family, although unexpressed and continually repressed, was, as we have seen, very strong in the holy Foundress, and while in the discharge of her duty there never was any half heartedness, still she could not entirely shake off the gloom that settled on her, and would not allow any celebration of the feast of her Patron Saint on the October following.

CHAPTER XXI

JOY BELLS IN THE AIR. ARCHBISHOP LYNCH'S JUBILEE

EARLY in Autumn, again the cloud was lifted, for the air was rife with preparations for the celebration of the Jubilee of that champion of education, Archbishop Lynch. Many visitors were expected to the city and decorations symbolic of religion and all that noble steadfastness implies, occupied the minds of religious artists and decorators. In the preparation of the musical programme by the children of the Abbey, Rev. Mother Teresa took the keenest interest, and Dr. Torrington, the famous musical director, was engaged to conduct the vocal numbers. On Wednesday, December 10th, '84, the Archbishop of Toronto, with a large number of Prelates and distinguished clergymen, arrived in Toronto by a special train from the Council of Baltimore which had been in session for some weeks, and they were met by a grand procession which escorted them to the Cathedral. In the evening there was a great display of fireworks. On Thursday, His Grace celebrated High Mass at the Cathedral, and the silver-tongued orator of the American hierarchy, Archbishop Ryan, of Philadelphia, delivered a panegyric on the life and virtues of the truly great Prelate, who had done so much for Catholicity in Toronto. On Friday, the Archbishop

230

accompanied by Bishop O'Mahoney, Archbishop Sweeney of Halifax, and Bishop Carberry of Hamilton visited the Abbey and received the Jubilee greeting of the pupils. He was always at home with the Abbey children, and he could not help noticing by the expression of their faces, their simple delight at the honours he was receiving on all sides, for that was the topic of the hour, and although they knew well that the little boys who generally escorted him in his visits and hung round his chair with the genuine admiration of the small boy for a great man, were his special favourites, still they were always stimulated to do their very best to merit his word of encouragement, which they treasured and prized. Indeed, Rev. Mother Teresa had on this occasion, as on many others, to curb the zeal of Mistresses and pupils to honour the distinguished guest, by omitting many parts of the elaborate programme, and childish aspirations went up from behind the scenes that various numbers on the programme might not be cancelled by the unerring hand, for on this special occasion every child wished to appear and take part in the entertainment.

Thus ended joyfully the year '84 and visits to the mission houses and Retreats occupied Rev. Mother's time very fully to the end of the scholastic year, and early in '85, although ailing from ear trouble and in many respects suffering bodily pain, we find her brave spirit and indomitable courage rising above physical ailments and consoling the lonely or downcast as the following letter which is typical of her enduring anxiety for all her children will show:

LORETTO ABBEY,
TORONTO, Feb. 25th, '85.

My Dearest S.M.M.,—

You may easily conceive how much concern I feel at hearing you are so lonely. I hope all this is a prelude to a great amount of good for yourself, and through you for others. Remember, dearest Sister M.M., that feeling is like the sea, ever changing, sometimes extremely stormy and besides most treacherous. It will cast you on rocks if you are not on guard. Those at sea often think that the roaring billows will surely swallow them up, and before long they find that all is calm and serene again. You must fix yourself on the rock of "Divine Will" against which the winds and waves beat in vain, and only serve to prove its stability. Pray and God will give you grace to rise above feeling which is merely natural and can be overcome by grace, which may be always obtained by prayer. If you allow yourself to be influenced by feeling, you cannot enjoy true peace. "The wise man built his house on a rock, and the winds blew and the rain fell, and the house was not overturned because it was built upon a rock." I know that nothing but prayer enables us to overcome feeling which though we may compare it to hysteria, is like a real suffering, if indulged. I heard a Jesuit once say, that feeling was given us to afford matter for sacrifice and should not be allowed to interfere with us. We may feel very badly yet be extremely fervent in the discharge of our duty, doing it because it is our duty, notwithstanding our feelings; that is real fervour, though we may be full of disgust naturally, and working hard against strong repugnances. I do hope, dearest Sister M.M., that you will soon be able to say that you are well and happy. Think of the poor Nuns in Egypt, what would they not give to be in your place? Try to get time to read the life of a Saint.

With much love after this dull sermon, I am ever,
Yours affectionately in C. J.,

M. J. TERESA.

This was her habitual trend of mind, and there was no suffering which did not appeal to her seemingly calm, unruffled spirit, and always with the idea of alleviating it, or if that was impossible, of praying for endurance for the sufferer. On March 20th, '85, came the first news of the outbreak of the rebellion among the half breeds and Indians of the Northwest. On the 26th of the same month, the first battle was fought at Duck Lake, on the 30th the troops left Toronto for the scene of action, among them brothers and relations of the pupils of the Abbey. After some skirmishes, a loss of sixty-six lives and one hundred and nineteen wounded was reported, and great consternation was felt all over the city for the fate of those who had obeyed the country's call "To Arms." A story was then current that two priests who had tried to persuade the Indians from rising, were murdered in cold blood and their hearts taken out and roasted before the eyes of the merciless rebels, and although Riel soon surrendered at Batoche, still the deepest anxiety was felt by friends in the east, lest the fiercer Indians, the Blackfeet, whom Rev. Father Lacombe had gone to visit in the meantime, would

233

also take the war path. The good missionary had taken up his abode with them at Gleichen, and remembering what his promises had meant to them in the past when he invariably caused the Government to see the justice of their claims, and procured for them the material aid they desired, they did not abuse his confidence, but kept to the ways of peace he counselled, and awaited the fulfilment of the promises of the Black Robe. He received the thanks of the Governor-General; and Protestants and Catholics in the then sparsely-settled Community of Alberta, united in honouring and thanking the Peacemaker. But in the east, party feeling ran high, and the rancour engendered by the tales of Indian atrocities excited the citizens, and this was very evident among the pupils. Rev. Mother Teresa was deeply moved by the manifestation of this feeling, but always silent; only when the subject was broached did she ever venture to speak of it, and then only to console those in trouble, but her prayer was incessant. On hearing a very bitter speech made by someone, whose indignation with the poor savages was great, she raised her eyes and said, "O, that poor woman, how I pity her!" Her few words had a very wonderful effect on those who heard her, and her serenity of countenance on that occasion, as on every other, suggested her union with God. In war or in peace, the duty to God was never allowed to be neglected, and in the succeeding calm, the processions of the Blessed Sacrament, the May devotions, the Closing Exercises, and the Retreats follow each other in quick succession. Then the frequent visitation of the mission houses occupied a great portion of her time, and although every one knew that her object in these visitations was not in any sense merely social or for change of scene, but for the purpose of acquainting herself with the manner in which God was served, and the Rules observed in the various houses of the Institute in America; still, her coming to any house was looked upon as a pleasurable event, and it was ever noted that she had the happy faculty of dissipating any distressful circumstance which might have previously existed. To a Superior, after having made the visitation of her house, she wrote:

LORETTO ABBEY, WELLINGTON PLACE,
TORONTO, (Undated).

My Dearest M.M.,—

Every day brings the conviction that we ought to be very kind to those whom God has confided to our humble charge. Father Baltazar Albarez says, "To be a Superior is to be the tutor of princes, to be the servant of the children of God; it is to have authority over men, but over free men, who have embraced servitude for the love of God." Never forget that those over whom you have authority are the Spouses of Jesus Christ, the temples of the Holy Ghost. What is feared is hated; what is hated is blamed, and blame weakens the feelings of confidence and respect. Still faults must be corrected, and can be more effectually when our general course with regard to others is kind. I do not think you are wanting in kindness, and I was glad to know the last time I was in ———— that you do not allow faults to pass with impunity. Wishing

you all that charity and peace which is God himself,
I remain,

Yours affectionately in C. J.,

M. J. Teresa.

On the 4th of May, '86, the Community in Lindsay
received a great blow in the death of their beloved
Bishop, Right Rev. Y. Jamot. Indeed, he had ever
been a kind father to the Nuns in his Peterboro'
diocese, and to Rev. Mother Teresa he was a friend
of the early struggling days in Toronto. He had been
Archbishop Lynch's loyal and devoted Vicar, and
knowing His Grace's esteem and friendship for the
Community, he treated the Religious with the same
paternal kindness as his Most Rev. Chief had done.
The blow was keenly felt by all, but to none did the
news of his demise bring more acute sorrow than to
the holy Foundress who could not help thinking that
the early friends of the Institute in Canada, and those
who from them had learned to value it, were being
removed one by one by the icy hand of death. But
her joys and sorrows have the same keynote of faith,
and she was never seen to grieve inordinately although
her sympàthies were deep, and in many cases not
fully expressed. Her gratitude, too, was marvellous;
most people express thanks either through courtesy or
genuinely, when touched by some mark of kindness
unusual or unexpected, but Rev. Mother Teresa
expressed gratitude sincere for receiving what was
legitimately her due. In the following letter she com-
bines gratitude with the kindly consideration which
each one came to feel was her due, when either

236

adversity or prosperity came to her. The relatives of the Nuns seemed to be adopted into her intimacy, and the ring of sincerity in her letters was often balm to a wounded heart as the following letter testifies:

LORETTO ABBEY,
TORONTO, 9th January, '88.

My Dearest S.M.M.,—

I received your kind letter, and I am very grateful to God and your dear honourable father, who so kindly and justly remembered your claim and the claim of God. May He reward him a thousand fold. I trust he is now enjoying the recompense of his holy integrity. R.I.P. I was pleased to hear from Mr. M.D., your throat is better and once more in good condition. Your school children, and those you get to go to instructions from the High School, will be gems in your immortal crown, D.V. I hope your visit cheered the dear ones at home. They have much to console them; and after the first great grief is over, their sorrow will be turned into joy.

With love to all, I am ever,

Yours fondly in J. C.,

M. J. TERESA.

To another she writes:

LORETTO ABBEY,
TORONTO, Feb. 13th, '88.

My Dearest S.M.M.,—

Your grief at the death of your very inestimable mother must be great naturally, but the grace of God

237

and your faith will sustain you, and enable you to
bear your greatest trial with resignation. The recollection of your dear mamma's virtues must fill you with
hope which, when the first anguish is over, will fill you
with joy. Your thoughts will henceforth be turned
Heavenward with more frequency and earnestness,
as what you loved best on earth is now in Heaven,
D.V.

We are all praying for your dear mamma, and I
have asked her to obtain a favour for me. I had a
most sincere esteem for dear Mrs. Hawkins; and so
must all have had who knew her. Your prayers and
virtues must supply her place in obtaining graces and
blessings for those in whom she and you were interested. R.I.P.

With much love and deep sympathy, I am ever,

Yours fondly in C. J.,

M. J. TERESA.

CHAPTER XXII

MOTHER CATHERINE OF THE PRECIOUS BLOOD. GRATITUDE OF THE FOUNDRESS. BUILDING AND NOT BUILDING.

GREGORY VII has been styled by some the greatest Pope because he had the greatest difficulties to overcome, and was undaunted in his work of purifying the church, and extending the kingdom of Christ; still he did not accomplish all he undertook, nor did he die after having apparently achieved a complete triumph. But his principles triumphed in the end and he broke the Hohenstauffen power infringing on the Papacy. Rev. Mother Teresa had difficulties of another kind to encounter, in commencing her religious career in a country, if not openly hostile to Catholicity, at least little in sympathy with it, or the spread of monasticism, and with her eyes ever eager for fields where the kingdom of Christ might be easily extended, she worked unceasingly in the land to which she had been called, a land somewhat sterile, or at least not very productive. What was her success? Will it ever be altogether known? We can safely affirm "No!" for while we have glanced over the foundations she made, we have omitted those to which she had been most cordially invited, as Brooklyn, Cornwall on the Hudson, Chatham, Chicago, and many others for which her heart yearned, but which paucity of vocations or some other circumstances equally deterrent, frustrated. Indeed, since her death, missions have been sent to places where the first invitations came from thirty years before, so that probably in Heaven she has caused to come to pass that which on earth she had to relinquish. In some cases application was made for a filiation by a Prelate who wished the Nuns to be diocesan, but as her motto ever was, "Union is strength," such an invitation could not be even considered, no matter how tempting the field, still it must have been some consolation to her in the early sixties that her little Community was so well and favourably known as to merit to be called on to labour in large Catholic cities, where many sought admission, for these large centres where many souls were to be saved, appealed strongly to her.

But perhaps more trying still was the case where no such impediment to the union of the body as a whole existed, but where the summons had to be immediately answered, though she had not subjects at the time, and the claims of education were pressing. Afterwards when she found herself in a position to send out a colony, a less desirable mission was offered and accepted. Material advantages did not weigh much in the balance with her, the saving of souls and the spiritual advantages enjoyed by the Religious largely determined her decision. Though as we have seen, hardships endured by the Nuns were keenly felt by her and a cross that came to any house of the Institute was specially her cross, and unlike the Cyrenian, she hastened to offer her assistance. In fact when she heard of any religious community having received a cross, her heart immediately went out to the sufferers, and whatever means were in her power to alleviate the distress, were promptly resorted to, although in some cases she could do nothing but pray, and that she did with an earnestness and sincerity that must have been pleasing to Almighty God. Her admiration for holy women of all states was often the theme of her conversation, and when she happened to meet one in the flesh who was known to have received some favours from God her delight was quite manifest. When the Precious Blood Nuns came to Toronto, and the fame of the sanctity of their holy Foundress, Mother Catherine, had preceded them, she was simply thrilled with joy at the hope of meeting her. When the saintly Foundress of the Precious Blood was Rev. Mother Teresa's guest at the Abbey, she was beside herself with gladness. Her face was radiant with pleasure, and the Mistress of schools was told to inform the young ladies of the sanctity of the Religious who was a guest of the Abbey with some members of her Community, until their own monastery was in a fit condition to receive them. At Mass the children wore their white veils as on feast days and Sundays, and sang a hymn of Thanksgiving, and after the Religious had been individually presented to this extraordinarily favoured Nun and received her blessing, the pupils of all the schools were brought forward that her kindly word of advice and benediction might be with them all through life. A holiday was granted to all the pupils in the morning and Rev. Mother Teresa was thoroughly pleased to hear how the young ladies treasured up each word spoken, and tried to extract something profitable from the advice Mother Catherine had given them. That was truly a red letter day at the Abbey,

16 T.D.

and when the two Foundresses sat side by side in the Reception room, Rev. Mother Teresa's children could not help thinking that they too had a Saint at their head, although the manifestation of the working of God in her case might be only judged from results. But nothing could be farther from Rev. Mother Teresa's thoughts on this day or on any other, for she had great humility, and indeed, the happiness of Mother Catherine's visit was a treasured memory all through life, for her esteem of the holy Nun grew as the years went by. Among the condolences offered to the Community by Prelates and Priests for the venerated Superior, there was none more prized than that of Mother Catherine, for whom she had such deep veneration. From Rev. Mother Teresa's attitude towards spiritual persons and things, one would almost deem her a mystic, but her Heavenly prudence and foresight were never lacking in affairs of business, and her point of view was almost always right. Writing to a Prelate who was represented to her as being desirous, that a rather expensive building should be constructed in his diocesan see, and with whom she evidently had some conversation on the subject. She writes: "I have given the project of building much consideration, since I had the honour of seeing Your Lordship, and have recommended it to God and St. Joseph. Besides this I have weighed the consequences of building and of not building, and I find that the first would be unjustifiable rashness, and the other will not, by proper arrangement, be attended with much inconvenience, and though it should, every foundation has to suffer a little in the beginning, though circumstances seem to have combined in favour of this one in your diocese, that it may almost be regarded as an exception to this general rule. Fearing that Your Lordship should think I have not done all in my power for the progress of N. Convent, I must assure you that I have sacrificed very materially the interests of Toronto in sending to N. a sister with whom we could very badly dispense, in fact, who was necessary for art, as our best Artist here, though superior to Sister M., had not the confidence of those she taught, owing to her being a Novice and a fellow pupil of those whom she afterwards instructed. Then the removal of Sister M. from the Falls was another step taken at great inconvenience for the benefit of N. It seems to me that there are many suggestions I can make to M.M. by following which she can easily make sufficient room for the boarders. Were you aware, my Lord, of all the money we owe, and the debts we must necessarily incur immediately, you would not allow, much less encourage, us to build at present."

But it was in building up the kingdom of God in souls that she was chiefly interested, and her sentiments may be gleaned in part from the following letter to a Superior in Ireland:

LORETTO CONVENT, 81 BOND ST.,
TORONTO, 18th January, 1888.

My Dear M.M.,—

You must feel deeply for poor M.M'.s affliction. I know your truly sympathetic heart, and how you grieve with those who grieve and rejoice with those who rejoice. May Our dear Lord give you cause to

243

rejoice always, both in time and eternity. Our missioners in the States are doing a great deal of good, and like all pioneers, are suffering some. I wish you could lend us some good Nuns for R. where we have been invited by Dr. B. Indeed, the thought of your sending a mission to the States, if you cannot to Australia, has often occupied my mind. God's Holy Will be done! May He direct you and us all to whatever will promote His greater honour and glory. Did you write to the Archbishop of Sydney? You have a sufficient number of Nuns to afford a mission but you must pray and weigh the step well. Our Lady of Angels and the angels of the Institute would be powerful helps in obtaining what we desire for the Institute. You may expect a visit from Miss C., a great friend of ours, whose mother as well as herself rendered great services to our Nuns in Stratford, and continues to do so. I send you an aspiration that is said to be very efficacious in obtaining what is asked. I am sure you write often to dear suffering Kate. I wish I could alleviate her sufferings by my unworthy prayers. I have no other means. Believe me, ever,

Yours affectionately in J. C.,

M. J. TERESA.

We have seen her well tempered zeal, and indeed, so long as good was done anywhere, she found consolation in the fact and in the knowledge of it. Her eyes were ever turned towards Heaven invoking blessings on the Community, or thanking God for the bestowal of them. For fine weather, good schools, the loan of money when she felt sure she could repay it, for all these and many other things she continually expressed thanks in a simple, natural way, and her joy over the entrance of the pupils in the early days when the harvest was great and the labourers few, was scarcely more marked than when in after years the children of some of the early pupils began to find their way to the Novitiate. On February 2nd, 1885, we find noted in a memorandum three sisters made their vows on this "feast of Our Lady" and after naming them she writes, "The last mentioned sister is the first member whose mother was a former pupil, to join our Community. Her aunts and mother were among the first who came to our school on Duke St. the day it opened, 29th September, 1847." Her conception of the virtues required for religious life is well illustrated in a letter written long before to one who became a brilliant member of the Order and kept sacredly as a treasure the advice she received from this most enlightened guide; until after her death, among her few earthly possessions was found in the very familiar writing of the Foundress, the instructions which were so faithfully carried out, and which ran as follows:

My Dearest H.,—

I feel much pleasure in acceding to your pious request. I rejoice to see you devote yourself so early to Him who alone is worthy of your whole heart. You may bear the glorious name of Loyola; render yourself agreeable to God by endeavouring to imitate the great Saint who made it venerable by his eminent virtures. Among these His humility and constant obedience should be your special aim. If you are humble and obedient, I can answer for your final happy perseverance in holy religion. Sister M.T. is in Toronto for a few days, she will return to Guelph on Friday next. I think the change of air will have done her some good by that time. The B. Nuns are in Retreat. I suppose you do not forget to pray for them. My first and last advice to you is to be humble. On this condition, according to the declaration of Truth Itself, you will have peace of soul which, next to God's holy grace, is Heaven's best gift. You see I already treat you as one of my own dear children by addressing to you this short but comprehensive exhortation. "Be thou faithful unto death and I will give thee the crown of life." Pray for me, dear H., and believe me,

Yours sincerely in J. C.,

M. TERESA DEASE.

CHAPTER XXIII

FINIS CORONAT OPUS. DEATH OF ARCH-BISHOP LYNCH. MOTHER JOACHIM MURRAY.

FOR some time in 1888, Rev. Mother Teresa's health was causing anxiety to the devoted Community that had been accustomed to consider her very existence almost essential to the great work she had in a measure inaugurated. But her visitations to the different houses of the Institute were as frequent, and her zeal, if anything, more pronounced than in the early days. It is true many spiritual guides of the struggling days, and some who had kindly continued their ministrations to the Community in later times, had been removed from the arena of the Church Militant. The Most Rev. Archbishop Lynch, who for over a quarter of a century had watched the growth of the Institute with a truly fatherly care and solicitude, worn out in the struggle for right, was fast showing signs of the running out of the sands of life. Probably the good he wrought has never been truly estimated and the blessings he procured for unborn generations, to whom his name will have no significance, are recorded in Heaven. It has been seen how his predecessor fought valiantly to secure Catholic schools for Catholic children, but on Mgr. Lynch's appointment to the see of Toronto, he had to continue the struggle until after Confederation, when mainly through his exertions the establishment of the Separate schools was an accomplished fact. In 1882 he had a very serious attack of erysipelas, and constant prayers were offered by the Community of Loretto for the prolongation of that life that seemed so necessary for the advancement of religion. On his recovery, when told of the earnest prayers that were offered in his behalf, he merely said, "I should have known that, even if I had not been told, but keep on praying for the success of my work." Six years later, when the final summons came, there was no time to pray for respite, for when word reached the Abbey of his mortal illness, and his express desire that the Loretto Nuns should be told of his extremity, he was already dead. The May was shrouded in mourning, and a true friend of Loretto, a champion of all good works, and a zealous defender of the Church, had gone to receive his reward. Rev. Mother Teresa had probably received the last great blow, which in the order of time she was to suffer, but the doctrine of the Communion of Saints was a consoling one for her, and suffrages were incessantly offered by the Community for the soul of its earliest, and staunchest friend.

Her unfailing faith in God's Providence was never more clearly shown than when the cross pressed most heavily, for from the annals we glean that at this time she redoubled her zeal for the spiritual welfare of the members of the Institute, and each night gave an exhortation on some one of the Rules, which, coming from the lips of one who had been styled by the spiritual director of many Retreats at Loretto, "the incarnation of Rules and religious observances," made an indelible impression. Of her first companions, the

248

true and tried, none remained at this time, even the first Canadian Postulant, Sr. M. Joseph McNamara, had already entered into her reward. But the first helpers, who in 1849 had come to the aid of the struggling little band of pioneer Nuns, were still busy at the harvest, and a word of the lifework of Mother Joachim Murray may not be out of place here. It has been recorded that Rev. Mother Teresa Dease, the third day after her holy profession, assumed the traveller's garb for the unknown land, but Mother Joachim Murray said good bye to her native land the very day she had made her vows. Brief indeed was the time that the snowy wreath of the Bride of Christ rested on her brow, for in a few hours after her solemn consecration to God, she left all that her heart held dear, and bade a life-long farewell to weeping friends, and on that fateful day, with a heart as pure and a soul as white as a babe's just baptized, began that journey previously related. But what was her life in the land of her adoption? Like the great Apostle, St. Paul, she became "all things to all men" that she might gain all to Christ. She came like a sunbeam from her Irish home to comfort and cheer the last months of Rev. Mother Ignatia Hutchinson's life, and afterwards to prove herself the life-long trusty friend of her successor, Rev. Mother Teresa Dease. In religious life, her bright intellect and rare ability, like the pure affection of her heart, were consecrated to the love and service of Jesus Christ, her Divine Master, and her whole life was consumed for His glory. Young, talented, simple and unworldly, full of charity, faith and goodness, her influence was so great that in

the schools her example had the magnetic effect of
drawing the hearts of the children to God. Indeed,
many of them saw the beauty of the Angelical life
and devoted themselves unreservedly to God's service
in religion, while, as has been before observed, some
who have had honourable careers in the world never
forgot her instructions, as was manifest in their conduct.

But not only the children of the schools, but the
poor, the sick and the helpless were the objects of her
solicitude. What a comfort she was to Rev. Mother
Teresa might be inferred from the various charges she
entrusted to her, and in each and all there was evidence of the obedience, simplicity and utter unworld-
liness which characterized her throughout life, but
the dear little soul had the faculty of exacting from
others the unquestioning obedience, which seemed to
be a virtue natural to her, in as large a measure as she
had practiced it herself. Indeed, one would find in the
life of St. Philip Neri many instances of the virtues
he required those under his direction to practice which
would remind one strongly of some of Mother
Joachim's favourite tests of solid virtue. A young
Religious, was anxious to spend the whole day in
the country and on the first opportunity her wish
was gratified, but she had to drive out with her
companion in a farmer's waggon, with the pleasant
companionship of a young calf. An order of this
kind was given with a kind smile and in such a
simple way that no one would feel that her virtue
was being tried, nor was she particular that acts
of this nature should always have an evidently

practical end. A Sister possessed of good understanding and an excellent disposition required to be taught simple obedience of will and judgment as Mother Joachim thought, and so one day when hastening to the school, she received word from her Superior, to empty a large quantity of flour from one barrel to another, but with a cup. The obedient Religious finished her task and remarked to a companion that it did not take such a fearfully long time as she had anticipated, only she regretted having crushed her nice guimpe which she had just put on a few minutes before she got the order. "Oh," laughed her companion, who was wearing a black veil, and had all the experience of the Novitiate, "perhaps that was partly the intention." Rev. Mother Teresa did not generally adopt the practices giving express orders to correct some fault, as her zealous daughter did, but heard with a great deal of pleasure how tasks entailing a good measure of mortification were generally performed with the greatest eagerness by Novices sincerely desirous to attain perfection. We have spoken much of Rev. Mother Teresa's great gift of sympathy, a slight trace of which may be detected in her letters, but this one gift Mother Joachim seemed to possess even in a greater degree. Rev. Mother Teresa's sympathy seemed to be felt more particularly for the members of the Community, their relatives, and the children entrusted to her care, but Mother Joachim seemed to exercise it in a wider sphere, for wherever she happened to be stationed, the sick and those in distress in the world soon found her out, and no one ever went away from her without receiving relief or comfort.

In the Community her charity was proverbial, and it was most manifest in her attitude to those whose suffering would not appeal so strongly to the majority. Towards a Sister whose malady inspired a feeling akin to fear in others, she was particularly compassionate, and she seemed to have a holy reverence for any one whom God had afflicted. Her duties of Infirmarian, Prefect of Health, and Librarian brought her into close contact with many, and there are those still living who can bear witness to her Christlike charity in office. The virtue of forgiveness she cherished, and children who had committed small faults and were in a way ostracized by being kept apart from the others some little time until they had acknowledged their fault, felt that in their temporary banishment they had at least one staunch friend.

Indeed, so well was this known to the Mistresses that they would not place a child to study or work in so-called punishment where Mother Joachim was likely to pass, but this did not prevent the offending juveniles from casting anxious glances towards the means of ingress or egress, for they were sure if she happened to be in the house at all, she must hear of their being in trouble, and that an immediate petition for pardon for the tiny offender would find its way to the school throne of forgiveness. Then a very wise word of counsel was given to the little culprit whose heart was already touched with gratitude towards the kindly intercessor, and invariably a friendship sprang up which had lasting effects. When a new day school was opened in after years, in a not very distant part of the city, it happened that some pupils who had attended the Bond St. Academy found it more convenient to pursue their studies in this new filiation, and during the recreation hours they contrasted their present quarters not altogether favourably with the old familiar Bond St. Convent, where many of their mothers had been pupils: What was lacking to their complete satisfaction was not very clear from their conversation until a tiny, mischievous little lass of ten piped out very audibly. "Well, there's no Mother Joachim here, so I shall take care not to break the Rules," and so Mother Joachim won her way into the hearts of the young and old with whom she had come in contact in Toronto until her death which occurred several years after the demise of Rev. Mother Teresa.

We have seen Rev. Mother Teresa's natural grief for the death of Archbishop Lynch, who had so nobly aided the Community in the early struggle, but the Foundress never pinned her faith to any individual for the ultimate success of a work all for God, and so the right of succession found in her a ready believer. "God will provide," was her motto when the days were longest and darkest, and now after having experiénced some of the sunshine of prosperity she did not hesitate to advance in the path which had been marked out for her, and to hope that God would raise up another upholder of the Institute when its position was more assured. In the meantime her interest in the Community was, if anything, more marked and the virtue of reliance on God and charity in the fullest sense of the word were becoming daily more evident. On one occasion in those latter years a Religious whose zeal, though never questioned, was somewhat severely criticised for the manner of its manifestation, found in her a firm defender. Not that she decided in an absolute way that the Sister's course of procedure was altogether wise, for it was not a question of right and wrong, but one of those subtle cases in which person's opinions are very decidedly maintained according to the point of view She had an innate horror of anything bearing the semblance of argument or controversy, seeing that no good end was served thereby, and therefore the difference of opinion, which seemed at the time to prevail, pained her exceedingly, but she was always strong enough to wait, and so began to adopt ways and means of restoring tranquility before taking a decisive step. Calling a Religious, who had just finished reading in the Refectory a chapter on "Fraternal Love and the beauty of Toleration," she took her into her confidence, and without blaming anyone, mentioned the fact that the seeming want of charity to one, on account of her personal opinion, deeply grieved her. The Religious felt particularly happy in being able to inform the Foundress that she had never uttered one word against the person whose lack of prudence was her greatest fault, when the Superior interrupted her by saying, "Could you not have gone further and spoken in her defence." Seeing her attitude, the Religious could not help remarking the imitation of the charity of the Master, and as events proved, the wisdom of the Foundress. And so it was always, the suggestion of the Divine was forever present to those who conversed with her, no matter what was the theme. Her very look was impressive though never constrained, and very few appeals were ever made from her judgment, when a decision was made, for that her view was God's view seemed to be taken for granted. Now, that view was not always very clear to all at first, but she had patience in an infinite degree, and waited until she had the full grasp of all sides of a question.

There was thought of removing a child from one of the schools, where her presence was not considered desirable for the others; and that the faults of the children should be known only to those who had witnessed them was her cardinal rule, except in very rare cases where the Superior had to be informed. So, after listening very patiently to the arraignment, she turned to the zealous Sister and said, "Have you ever made the invincible Novena for this child? Well, commence it." This Novena consisted of forty "Our Father's" recited during Mass, and as the interview took place at the closing of school, during the whole summer vacation, the prayer was repeated with, we hope, salutary effects. In her whole intercourse with the Community and others, there was never any visible deviation from the dominating thought of personal sanctity and zeal for souls, and no one who ever came under the sphere of her influence in an intimate way could completely cast off the remembrance of an unseen power which was thoroughly felt.

One cold, frosty morning, when the day pupils were speedily wending their way to the Abbey, they were closely followed by a young woman apparently demented, but who seemed to be possessed with the one idea of not losing sight of the affrighted children.

REV. MOTHER TERESA DEASE

On they came, faster and faster, and still more closely pursued until they reached the gate, when a scream uttered simultaneously brought the young ladies' Refectorian, who was working on the ground floor, to the entrance. The children held their breath for fear, but their glances to the rear revealed the object of their dismay. There the poor woman stood in her bare feet, in the deep Canadian snow, with a look of unconcealed triumph that she had reached the goal. The pupils hastily scattered to their class rooms and spread the report that a crazy woman had followed them and forced an entrance into the building. All was disorder and dismay, when some Sisters who had come on the scene went to the room indicated where she had entered, and begged the poor frantic woman to be seated and rest awhile, but no, she became violent, her body was bruised and wounded from having jumped from a two story window to the street. Suddenly Rev. Mother Teresa appeared at the Refectory door and in an instant the poor creature cried out, "The Blessed Virgin!" and advanced towards the bewildered Superior, who gently led her to a chair, and seating herself beside her coaxed her to have her feet washed and to put on shoes and stockings. After some time she helped her to some food, and the poor insane woman, with her eyes fixed on her ministering angel, gratefully partook of what was offered her, and revealing her name, promised that she would return peacefully home when her father, who could not sufficiently express his thanks to those who had sheltered his child, was summoned to take her away.

Rev. Mother Teresa's holiness of life became more

256

visible as she neared the Eternal Shore, and her naturally grave deportment was relieved by an expression
of countenance which suggested some communication
with a better world. Nor was the sense of humour,
before remarked, altogether lacking in those days
when her work might be looked on as almost completed, as the following incident will show. Not only
for the Novices who might be looked on as her direct
spiritual children, but for the pupils in the schools,
was her zeal unabated. One of the pupils was reported
to her as incapable of studying or learning anything,
and as the young girl had been carefully prepared for
the reception of the Sacraments, it seemed as if nothing further could be done for her. Until this religious
instruction had been thoroughly attended to, Rev.
Mother made no inquiries about her accomplishments
or the extent of her education, but after she had
received the Sacraments regularly, and was a practical
Catholic, Rev. Mother thought some more particular
attention should be given to other instruction of the
boarder. She discovered, personally, that she had a
rather pleasing voice and received some special vocal
training. Then she advanced Carlyle's Theory in her
regard, that a person may learn almost anything by
intelligent reading. To the Religious to whom the
Foundress advocated this theory, it was a revelation,
for she never heard her quote Carlyle before, but it
served her purpose that time, for she arranged that
one of the very best readers should take the girl
privately, and have her read to her for a specified time
every day. The work was delightedly undertaken by
the Religious, and as the pupil had some elocutionary

17 т.ᴅ.

ability, the instructress flattered herself that she had an easy task to perform, and hastened to inform Rev. Mother of an assured success. The smile which had something of the Divine in it, was the pledge of her reward. Nevertheless she did not come soon again to reassure her Superior. Rev. Mother knew that the Nun went to her allotted task cheerfully, but after some time she questioned her on results, when the still undaunted Religious replied, "Rev. Mother, she would read beautifully if she knew the words." At this simplicity, Rev. Mother Teresa laughed outright and said gently, "Why, that's the trouble, get her to know the words." In after days, Rev. Mother pleasantly remarked if anyone read badly, "She would read, as Sister M.M. says, beautifully, if she only knew the words!" The teacher had to learn that her task was not such an easy one, and the mastery of words which she had taken for granted was in some cases rather difficult.

Rev. Mother Teresa kept in touch with even slight matters, and this not only in the Mother House, but in the missions, where her presence was cordially hailed by Nuns and children. Her keen eye detected signs of a vocation where another would sometimes form a totally different opinion of the possessor, and if the religious state was not embraced, she invariably alleged the Religious were somewhat at fault.

Visiting a class exhibition in one of the convents during her sojourn in that mission house, she remarked a particularly bright girl who at the time was also rather troublesome, but Rev. Mother's presence seemed to be an inspiration to the young lady on that occasion, for her answers were so accurate and her reasoning so clear that even her teacher marvelled. After class was over, Rev. Mother observed to the Mistress, "Miss N. has a religious vocation!" This opinion was received with respect but with some doubt, as the young lady had previously shown no liking for religious life nor discipline, but the clear mind, enlightened by grace, asserted itself, and in a short time after, she called at the Abbey to bid Rev. Mother Teresa good bye before entering the contemplative Community to which she felt she had been called. Rev Mother's old admiration and affection for the young girl were revived, and although she longed to have this rare jewel set in Loretto's crown, still the desire was never expressed but visibly felt. The promising pupil, in her chosen field, attained to heights of sanctity, and gladly marched on even to Calvary, for when her own devoted mother, by some means or rather circumstances, obtained access to her bedside when she was dying, and tried to alleviate her sufferings, the generous soul quoted the example of her beloved Spouse, Who on the cross had no balm for His wounds. Rev. Mother heard from one of her friends with what resignation, one might almost say gaiety, the sufferings of this young contemplative were borne, and tears, not of regret but of joy, filled her eyes on hearing of the transference of the pure soul to the Heavenly kingdom. Such were some of the joys that came to her at sunset, for with the eyes of faith, she regarded them as the heralds of the near dawn.

What then did Rev. Mother Teresa do for Catholic education in those days in that city which was the mecca of her hopes in early youth? The words of Rev. Father Francis Ryan, at one time the Catholic representative in the Senate of Toronto University, spoken at the Jubilee celebration of Loretto Abbey, might perhaps afford the best answer. He said, on that auspicious occasion, "This appreciative and cultured audience, all pupils or friends or patrons of Loretto, is eloquent by its presence of work well done. And a most interesting sketch of the Institute in the Jubilee number of the "Leaflets" tells the touching and instructive story of Loretto's life and work all over the world. What then is left for me to say? I think I may find two thoughts in the Magnificat of Loretto that have not been fully expressed, the true character of Christian education, and how this education is given in a Catholic Convent. These thoughts will be appropriate for what may be rightly called a Jubilee of Catholic education. I lately heard a definition of education from one of the leading educators of this country and I must confess it amazed me, especially as it was given before the cultured men in Toronto, the members of the Senate of our University. "Education is the formation of character, the fitting of a man for social, civil, and political life," and by man he was careful to say he meant homo which includes the woman, too. Now the strange thing about this definition is that it does not contain the slightest reference to God or eternal life, although the man who gave it is a Minister of religion. Our definition of education is the complete harmonious development of all the faculties and powers of the mind and heart of man, in due subordination to his destined end, the salvation of his soul and the glory of God. So says plainly our Magnificat of Loretto, "My soul doth magnify the Lord" gives us the principal, the ideal, the adequate object of true education, and "My spirit rejoiceth in God, my Saviour" gives us the end and the means of best and highest moral culture. The education of a human being must be mental and moral, the education of the mind and the education of the heart. Man is a religious as well as a rational animal and his education must be in keeping with his nature. Man was made for God and his education should enable him to know his last end and to attain it. The first principle of all true education is laid down by St. Ignatius, the illustrious founder of one of the greatest educational societies the world has ever seen. Man was created to praise, reverence and serve God, and by so doing to save his soul. This is the principle implied in the Magnificat, and this is the principle that is perfectly carried out in the educational system of Loretto. Mental and moral culture is their programme, the education of the mind and the heart. Their motto is "Ad Majorem Gloriam Dei," "To the greater glory of God." "Glory to man in the highest, for man is the measure of things," sings the agnostic poet of the nineteenth century. And our secular and scientific educationists answer, "Amen." "Glory to God in the highest," sang the angels, "for God is the Maker and Master of things," and so sing and say the first Lady of Loretto and all her children in the educational work of forming character and of saving souls. But characters are not formed nor souls saved by knowledge only. The education of the intellect is necessary but not sufficient. What is needed now, what was always needed, is the education of the heart. The intellect thinks, the will acts, the mind reasons, the heart loves. Man is not saved by thinking or by reasoning or by concluding or even by acting. He is saved, with God's help, by loving. "Thou shalt love the Lord, thy God." "My child, give me thy heart." The Ladies of Loretto are admitted by the most competent authority in Canada to hold the first rank as teachers; they are nearly all certificated teachers of highest class. But secular authority, no matter how competent and efficient, certificates, no matter how high, would never qualify them for true Christian teachers unless they had graduated in the school of Christ, and they have. What they and their friends rejoice at to-day, is not that they hold first place in educational work of highest order all over the world, but it is that they have won this proud distinction, not so much by their talents, industry, and excellent educational methods, as by their heroic sufferings in the great cause of Christian education." In closing, the Reverend orator gave a brief sketch of the Institute and its work in England, Ireland and Canada. He paid a glowing tribute to the three great Foundresses: Mother Mary Ward in England, Mother Teresa Ball in Ireland, and Mother Teresa Dease in Canada. But a tree is best known by its fruit and the Loretto Abbey Alumnae Association, formed in the golden jubilee year of Loretto Foundation in Toronto, might answer our question quite as satisfactorily. In "Leaflets from Loretto" in 1900 Mrs.

FINIS CORONAT OPUS

Emma O'Sullivan says, "Loyalty cannot be satisfied until it gives expression to its sentiments. It is not surprising then that the old pupils of Loretto—those of the early days of struggle and trial, and those of the later days of attainment and ease, embrace enthusiastically the occasion given by Loretto's Jubilee to form themselves into an association whose existence would be an eloquent testimony of the loyal love, the children of Loretto bear their Alma Mater, and a declaration of interest in all who have shared or still enjoy its motherly guidance." The time was all too short to do more than elect Officers of the Alumnae Association of Loretto, and to name an executive body to act with them. These Officers were:

Hon. President—Mrs. Plunkett, Ottawa.

President—Mrs. E. McDonnell, Port Huron, Mich.

Vice-Presidents—Mrs. John Foy, Toronto; Mrs. Dwyer, Toronto.

Secretaries—Miss Mary E. Mason, Toronto; Mrs. Scales, Toronto.

Mrs. McDonnell, on account of the distance of her place of residence from Toronto, requested Mrs. Emma O'Sullivan to act for her. Miss Mason resigned on account of absence from the city; Miss Alma Small was appointed in her place. These Officers were truly representative types of the results of Reverend Mother Teresa's teaching, nearly all of whom had come under her direct influence, and indeed, they embraced the period of struggles and trials for Loretto as well as the period of attainment and ease in a comparative sense which followed, for not only in their Alma Mater are they well and favourably known, but in

263

social life their example has been felt and far reaching influence spread for the betterment of the world. Their names are well known to the poor in their homes, and to those who struggle for the best things in life their aid has not been wanting, whilst in their families they are held in benediction. If Rev. Mother Teresa had seen that assembly presided over by the first Loretto pupil in Canada who was destined to take her place as Rev. Mother Ignatia, she might have said with greater reason than the mother of the Gracchi, "These are my jewels." But this is in anticipation and although without doubt a result of her labour if not directly, at least indirectly through the Nuns whom she had formed.

The Superior of a well known Order, passing through a place about the last year of the life of the Foundress, visited Loretto Convent and on her departure, surrounded by a group of the Religious who had accompanied her to the gate, remarked that they all seemed very faithful copies of their Mother. When this was related to the holy Foundress she remarked with the ready wit that never forsook her, "Yes, faithful copies of Mother Eve." Her zeal for their perfection as Religious educators never abated in the least, and to the last year of her life a word mispronounced or a provincialism thoughtlessly used by a Religious would be sure to fall on no unheeding ear and would not pass uncorrected. Sometimes, indeed, a look would be sufficient to remind the Nuns that there was something faulty in language or manner or address, and to remedy the fault as one expressed it, "before it was indelibly stamped on Rev. Mother's memory," seemed to be the only way to make her forget the offence against good taste. A member of a Commission who had been sent from Overseas to investigate educational conditions in the large cities of Canada and the United States remarked, "I judge systems by results, and the basis of my classification is the reverence of the youth in these large centres." Well, reverence for all human beings since each had an immortal soul and more especially for those invested with authority, may be styled the keynote of all the instructions of the Foundress to the Religious.

But reverence for God's Holy Name was a most marked attribute of the Foundress, and many years after her death, when the procession in honour of the Holy Name marched from St. Michael's Cathedral to the Abbey grounds for Benediction, one could not help feeling that in Heaven she rejoiced. The numbers of reverent Catholic men and boys, who in orderly ranks passed through the Abbey gate on that memorable Sunday, equalled the number of the whole population of Toronto when the Nuns came there in 1847. Monsignor McCann and Very Rev. Dean Hand were among the earliest arrivals, and the Monsignor waited until every available inch of ground was covered by living humanity before he bore the Blessed Sacrament through the winding walks to the temporary Altar erected, round which the multitude, with bowed heads, assisted at Benediction. This worthy priest had officiated at Religious ceremonies and presided over many functions at the Abbey in the past, and on this solemn occasion he performed his last, most notable ministration. As Chairman of the Separate School Board and parish priest of St. Mary's, as well as at times Administrator of the diocese, he was always a true friend to Loretto, and a tie will always bind him to the Community, for his beloved niece, who now rests in the cemetery, was a brilliant graduate of 1893, and afterwards Superior of Loretto Convent, Sault Ste. Marie.

CHAPTER XXIV

THE END

AS we have seen, towards the end of the eighties the physical strength of Rev. Mother Teresa was a source of anxiety to the Religious who were nearest to her, but to those who were on the missions scarcely a word might be said on the subject which would not cause misgiving if not real alarm. There was scarcely any outward change except an increased zeal for souls and a more marked care for regularity and religious discipline. On the occasion of her last visit to Joliet a priest who had called on her on business regarding the parochial schools and was going away perfectly satisfied, remarked, "Well, it is a great pity, but I do not expect to see that lady again. However, I am glad I had this interview with her. It seems to have done me good." "Why, Father F.," a Nun replied, "she will be here next year again." "No," he replied, "she is visibly dying. You do not seem to notice her extreme pallor." When it was remarked to the Foundress that the priest expressed satisfaction regarding the object of his visit, she merely said, "Oh, the humility of that priest!" and so it was always with her. She scarcely ever failed to detect virtue, although by no means given to inordinate praise, and it was with Communities as with individuals. In one of her journeys from the West, she stayed at a very poor, small convent, and her assistant, Rev. M. Ignatia, observed to her how edifying the poverty of the Nuns

267

was, when to her surprise Rev. M. Teresa went into details and said how well they had decorated their pretty little Chapel, and how spotlessly clean and inviting the whole place was.

Then from her letters quoted before we find her in perfect admiration of some of the largest communities of New York, the Sacred Heart, which she visited on her journey to Ireland and where she was edified beyond measure by the recollectedness of the Religious, and the spiritual atmosphere of the place, and so, the Convents in Europe of her own order, and the famous Ursuline Convent of Blackrock. The sorrows of the poor grieved her and even from the Old Land, from which she had obtained many substantial gifts of money and value for her struggling Community in early days from those who were her relatives and personal friends, the cry of those less fortunately situated did not reach her in vain, for she knew how to intercede for them with those who could aid. Towards the beginning of April it could be seen that her journeys by land and sea were over, and just as she began to see fruit on all the branches of the tree she had planted, it became evident she would not see many more harvests. She could look round after forty years of missionary life, and behold the many Convents and schools she had established, placed on a firm basis, the thousands of children being educated by the Nuns, and the personal respect and esteem felt for her by those whose opinions were valued. Indeed, in her case this feeling of respect was universal, and from the correspondence of persons in different walks of life we shall select letters which will bear testimony to the feel-

ings of genuine veneration she inspired. Then her visits
to the Blessed Sacrament in the spring of '89 became
more frequent and longer, and her step, always measured, became slower, but it were heresy yet to mention
to any of her spiritual daughters a surmise that the
end was near. However, some of her Nuns wrote
to those on the distant missions that it was feared she
was slowly dying. In any letters written by her at
that time, there was no hint of her own physical suffering, and so in that last spring of her existence we
find her writing to a suffering Sister, who had evidently
been cured by a miracle, as this Religious still living,
handed in the little faded sheet in the well known hand,
just at the termination of this sketch, and in it there
is not the slightest intimation of any concern for her
own health, but, as usual, intense solicitude for others.

It runs thus:

LORETTO CONVENT,

NIAGARA FALLS, 2nd Feb. '89.

M.R.A.

My Dearest S.M.M.

I was longing very much to hear from you or of you,
and Sr. M. Theodora's letter told me you were better.
D.G.

With regard to the promise, dear, good Father
Dumortier suggested, I would say, promise to abstain
from pork on Wednesdays; this will be a little mortification and sufficient when done through obedience.
I left Sr. M. A. in Hamilton, full of fervour and quite
hopeful for your cure, but satisfied with God's Will
which is always good and the *best*. The sleighing is
very pleasant. It would just suit you, it is so easy

and smooth, very much more so than driving in a carriage with wheels. A change back to Toronto might serve you now. I will hear from you before I determine on your return.

With much love to all, I am,

Ever yours fondly in C.J.

M. J. Teresa.

Just before her death came the following letter from the Bishop of London who had known her well from the early struggling days:

Bishop's Palace,
London, June 12th, 1889.

Dear Reverend Mother:

I have heard with very great sorrow of your serious illness, but hope that it will pass away as did similar attacks in the past. In any case I am sure you are quite resigned to the Holy Will of God and that you put your hope and confidence in Our Divine Lord Whom you have been serving for so many years in Religious life. "I know Whom I have believed," said Saint Paul, "and I am sure He is able to keep that which I have committed to Him against that day." "Yes, Our Blessed Lord is Bountiful to reward, and most merciful to forgive. Hence St. Peter tells us to cast all our cares, all our pains and trials upon Him, for He hath charge of us." Put your utmost confidence, therefore, in Our loving Saviour, Whose delight is to make His faithful servants eternally and infinitely happy. I pray for you every day, and I trust that whether you stay here yet awhile, or in the great

THE END

Hereafter, you will not fail to remember my interests before God. I would gladly go down to see you were it not for the many engagements I have to meet in the various parishes.

Wishing you God's abundant graces and blessings, I am,

Your sincere friend,

+ John Walsh, Bp. of London.

Letter from Rt. Rev. R. O'Connor, D.D.:

Bishop's House,
Peterboro, June 20th, 1889.

Mother Ignatia.

Dear Mother:

Lately I heard that Rev. Mother Teresa was very ill and in danger. Would you please tell her that I send her my blessing and that occasionally I remember her in my Masses? Ever since I first became acquainted with her I have had the greatest esteem for her great piety, and the many other virtues that have shone so pre-eminently in her life. Doubtless the crown which our Divine Lord has reserved for her must be very brilliant.

Wishing all the Nuns the choiest blessings from the Sacred Heart of Our Lord,

Believe me,

Yours in XT.,

R. A. O'Connor,
Bp. of Peterboro.

271

Weeks and days went by without any sign of improvement, and still not a murmur escaped her, nor did the hope of the Nuns wane that a miracle might be wrought in her favour. So, while employing the most enlightened medical skill, Divine aid was sought through the intercession of holy persons, and the prayers of those thought to be most pleasing in the eyes of God. Finally the Last Sacraments were received with the devotion and faith which were the marked attributes of her whole life. The diligence and care which she bestowed on the house of God as she styled every part of the Convent, showed strongly in those last days, and it was only when Vicar General Rooney addressed her in his strong words of faith that she had done with earth, that she gave up the supervision of all earthly concerns. "Let your thoughts and conversation be henceforth in Heaven, Reverend Mother," he said solemnly, and, like a true follower of the obedient Son of God, she never after referred to any temporal matter. The Nuns from the nearer missions came to see her for the last time, and there, on her bed of death, she welcomed them with the old smile, and followed their retreating figures with eyes bespeaking a benediction. Two holy Priests still living, and doing great things for God in widely different spheres, visited her on the last day, and prayed over and blessed the dying Religious, whose eyes to the last revealed her grateful appreciation of spiritual blessings. Those who were near her on that most solemn occasion will never forget her last act of contrition and humble prayer for pardon ere her lips were sealed and her eyes were closed forever on that memorable July 1st, 1889.

THE END

We draw a veil over the scene of desolation in that house which she had transformed from a bower of worldly gaiety into the temple of God. In spirit we might attend at the grand Requiem chanted, and follow the obsequies, at which were present Right Rev. Bishop Dowling of Hamilton, Right Rev. Bishop O'Connor of Peterboro, and Right Rev. Bishop O'Mahoney, Auxiliary of Toronto, besides numerous clergy and members of the Religious Orders. Vicar General Rooney celebrated Mass, assisted by Rev. Father Hand as Deacon and Rev. Father Kiernan as Subdeacon. Afterwards, Father Rooney, the Administrator, delivered the sermon, referring to the life work of the deceased Mother in eulogistic words. At the conclusion of the services, the pallbearers bore the coffin to the hearse in waiting, while the Sisters and visitors, with lighted tapers, knelt along the route to the convent gate. The remains were conveyed to Niagara Falls on the 12.20 train, accompanied by a special draped car conveying those in attendance, the pallbearers, Religious and several Priests who formed an escort. They were met at the Niagara Depot by M. Regis Harris, of Loretto Convent, Niagara Falls, and M. Eucharia Magann, Superior of Joliet, at the time. On the arrival of the party at Niagara, pallbearers from Niagara Falls joined in the procession, the Toronto pallbearers following next to the remains; then came the Priests, and after them the Religious, in all making a very solemn funeral cortege. The line of carriages slowly wended its way around the banks of the majestic Niagara, over which she had so often driven in her visits of charity and love, to the Loretto

18 T. D.

REV. MOTHER TERESA DEASE

Convent overlooking the Cataract. Then the remains were borne up the broad stone steps to the Chapel where all that was mortal of the saintly Foundress lay until the last solemn Requiem was chanted at 10.30 on the morrow. The last solemn procession was formed of all her spiritual children present, to the little cemetery on the grounds where she rests to await the final call. The following lines by one of her saintly daughters, Sr. M. Ignatia Downey, since deceased, record the feelings of the Religious for their departed Mother:

IN LOVING MEMORY
OF REV. MOTHER TERESA DEASE,
Superior General
OF THE INSTITUTE OF THE BLESSED VIRGIN IN AMERICA,
WHO DIED AT LORETTO ABBEY, TORONTO,
JULY 1st, 1889.

Toll sadly ye bells of the Cloister,
The soul of our loved one has flown.
Toll sadly! and echo the sorrow
Of hearts that are weary and lone!
For death's darksome shadow is o'er us
It shrouded us all in its gloom
And the form of our dear sainted Mother
Is robed for the cold silent tomb!

We gaze on the sweet pallid features
Now stamped with stern Death's icy seal,
And God alone knoweth the sorrow,
The anguish her orphan ones feel;

THE END

No more shall those eyes look upon us
No more shall we hear that sweet voice
Which as sounds of some liquid-like music
Made the hearts of her children rejoice.

It soothed every trial and sorrow
With sweet, gentle accents of love
Its tone seemed to draw down upon us
The spirit of peace from above.
But the smile that was light in our darkness
Is still on the pale lovely face
Which ever in life seemed to mirror
Her soul's spotless beauty and grace,

Ah! calm be thy rest, dearest Mother,
For well was thy life's labour done,
And closely thou followed thy Jesus
Till Zion's bright glory was won!
The works of thy zeal shine resplendent
More bright than the world's proudest fame,
And high in the archives of Heaven
Have angels recorded thy name.

Thou'lt live in the hearts of thy children
As long as life's journey shall last,
And they live in the fond, holy memories
Of the sweet saintly life that is past!
Nor time with its ruthless destroying
Shall dim the remembrance so dear,
Of virtues, that like crystal fountains
E'er sparkled before us so clear.

REV. MOTHER TERESA DEASE

Alluring us onward, still onward
To paths that thy saintly feet trod
The light of thy holy example
E'er leading us nearer to God.
Then still lead us onward, dear Mother,
For dark seems the way without thee,
But Mary, thy Guiding Star ever
Thy children's consoler shall be.

And mid the hot tears that are falling
As sadly we breathe our "Farewell"
We raise our dim eyes to the glory
Which human tongue never can tell;
And angels, seem whispering softly
"When earth's weary exile is o'er,
In Heavenly joys never ending
You'll meet your loved Mother once more."

Guelph, July 8th, 1889.   "LORETTO."

THE END

From the much revered Pastor of St. Patrick's, Montreal, Rev. Father Dowd, came the following kind words :—

ST. PATRICK'S,
MONTREAL, July 3rd, 1889.

Rev. Mother Assistant :—

I have just received the news of your Rev. Mother's death. I am grateful for your attention in giving me this early notice of an event which is as sad for the children as it joyful for the Mother. I am sure she has gone to her well earned reward in Eternity. I have seldom met a Religious who had the spirit of her calling in the same degree of perfection she had. She was governed habitually by a spirit of faith, of simplicity and of fervent love for God, and an anxious desire to see her Community work alone for the honour and glory of God.

You have my full sympathy in your great loss, though I am convinced that you have gained an intercessor in Heaven to replace a Mother on earth. Pray for me, and believe me,

Very sincerely yours in J. XT.,

P. DOWD, Priest.

REV. MOTHER TERESA DEASE

Letter from the father of two pupils :—

DALY AVENUE,
OTTAWA, July 4th, 1889.

Dear Mother Ignatia :—

I beg leave to offer you and through you to the Community the heartfelt sympathy and condolence of my little circle and myself, upon the death of the good and saintly Rev. Mother Teresa. How you will miss her wise counsel, her experience and her loving guidance we who have had the privilege and happiness of her acquaintance for the last thirty-three years can easily understand. Those alone who enjoyed her friendship and companionship can realize her loss. But it may truly be said your loss is her gain, and it will be consoling to know, that she can now do more for her dear Loretto, with Him Whom she served so long and so faithfully, than she accomplished in the exalted and responsible position which she occupied for so many years with such marked success, and to the admiration of all who knew her. Be assured, dear Mother, our unworthy prayers shall be offered for the eternal repose of her pure soul. The girls are not at home, but I hope they will write to express the sorrow I know they feel for one who was their true friend, and for whom they have entertained the greatest respect, and admiration ever since they acquired sense and judgment enough to estimate her worth and excellent qualities.

THE END

With the renewed assurance of our sympathy, and kindest regards to yourself and the other Ladies of our acquaintance, I remain,

Dear Mother Ignatia,

Sincerely yours,

JAMES G. MOYLAN.

REV. MOTHER TERESA DEASE

Reverend Mother Teresa's Grave at Niagara Falls.

High o'er the fast flowing river,
That leaps from its bed with a bound,
Nigh where the wild rapids shiver
There rises a green stately mound,
Whose sides lofty shade trees adorn
And willow and mountain ash wave
Their branches from bright sunny morn
To-night, o'er our dear Mother's grave.

Years have gone by since she left us,
The waters look glad as before,
And echo has not bereft us
The rime of the Cataract's roar.
The ruddy sun rises at morn,
O'er rocks that the rude waters lave
And bathes with a brightness newborn
The sod o'er that sweet sainted grave.

Now gone are the rose tints of dawn,
In haste to the west sweeps the sun,
Black shadows flit o'er the green lawn,
Since day-star's swift course had begun
Why follow such fleeting glory
O'er mountain, o'er valley, o'er wave,
More bright is the light of life 's story,
Shot back from the cross on that grave.

THE END

Letter from Mother Catherine Aurelie, Foundress of the Order of the Precious Blood, to:—

Reverend Mother Ignatia,
Loretto Abbey, Toronto.

Rev. Mother :—

I have just learned that you are an orphan—that your venerated mother is in Heaven. Although I am nearly at the moment of my departure I do not wish to withdraw without having expressed to you quick and profound sympathy, and without having assured you that my prayers and my sacrifices intercede for you with God as well as for each of the dear afflicted ones of your house.

In our mutual sorrow let us raise our eyes to Heaven; the one whom we have lost enjoys its happiness. She possesses the God she has so much loved, and she rests in His bosom from her long sufferings. There she will remember us, above all, those who were her spiritual daughters, and whom she loved with such maternal tenderness. It is from there she will watch over them, and she will bless them with a benediction quite specially efficacious. It is there she will prepare for each one a place near her, and while awaiting the day of the eternal reunion she will beg for them graces and blessings from on high.

Courage then, my dear Reverend Mother! Equal courage to all her beloved children! All the Community unites with me to pray for the soul of the venerated Mother who has just left you, and for the afflicted Religious who bewail her loss, in order that to her may

281

be accorded the sight of God in His glory if she does not already enjoy it, and that to her children the sight of God across the transparent veil of Trial may be equally perceptible.

Calling down on you the benedictions of the Blood of Jesus and the light of the Holy Ghost, I remain with deepest sympathy,

Reverend and dear Mother,

Your very humble and quite sympathetic friend,

SISTER CATHERINE AURELIE,
Superior.

Warwick Bro's & Rutter, Limited, Printers and Bookbinders, Toronto, Canada.